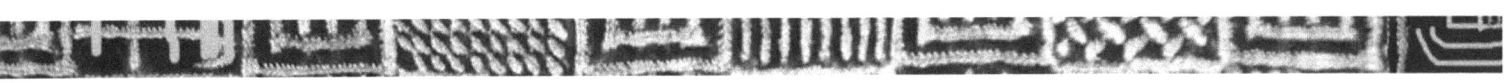

THE ULTIMATE GUIDE TO IGBO PLANTBASED COOKING AND HEALING

IGBO VEGAN

Copyright ©2021 Nena Ubani.
All rights reserved. First paperback edition published 2021in the United Kingdom.
A catalogue record for this book is available from the British Library.
ISBN 978-1-913455-36-1
No part of this book shall be reproduced or transmitted in any form or by any means,
electronic or mechanical, including photocopying, recording, or by any information retrieval system
without prior written permission of the publisher.
Published by Scribblecity Publications.
Printed in Great Britain.
Although every precaution has been taken in the preparation of this book,
the publisher and author assume no responsibility for errors or omissions.
Neither is any liability assumed for damages resulting from the use of this information contained herein.

*Dedicated to the memory of my late mother, **Nwakaego**.
I am because she was.*

"A man who calls his kinsmen to a feast does not do so to save them from starving. They all have food in their own homes. When we gather together in the moonlit village ground it is not because of the moon. Every man can see it in his own compound. We come together because it is good for kinsmen to do so."

- *Chinua Achebe, Things Fall Apart*

FOREWORD

"You're a Nigerian Vegetarian? You mean you don't eat meat?" My facial expression and tone of voice echoed my shock and amusement at encountering a Nigerian Vegetarian. The year was 2001, veganism was not trending and at the time nothing seemed more far-fetched, inconceivable, and amusing than the conversation I was having with a Nigerian vegetarian!

We were at a house party (a regular occurrence in Nigerian communities), the sounds and smells of 'party food' suya, fried fish, moi moi, mixed meat vegetable soup and stews were all around us. My son was with me, and we joked and laughed a lot with our new vegetarian friend. Between mouthfuls of meat dishes, we curiously questioned our new friend about what she could eat and why she was vegetarian. To me as a Nigerian this was a bit weird, "not a thing", "not done" it seemed like eccentric western ideology. Before leaving the party, we humorously wished her a speedy recovery from her vegetarian challenge.

Fast forward 5 years and I find myself not eating meat but also not eating any animal-based foods. From laughing at a Nigerian Vegetarian, I had now become a Nigerian Vegan which is someone who only eats plant-based products: No milk, no fish, no butter, no eggs, no products that come from an animal. How did I get to this point you may wonder? The simple answer is ill health. I had become ill and all allopathic medicine had to offer me was medication to manage my symptoms. When my family and I changed our lifestyle and became vegan we obtained natural nutritional relief from medical conditions that were merely being serviced via prescriptions.

As I stated in a recent 2020 article - *"Being Black and Vegan is Nuanced"*. Africans were a mostly plant-based people before the colonial era. It has been a great pleasure, a comfort and a heart-warming experience to read through the recipes in this book. I was transported back to being a young child, running around with friends while adults cooked up a storm in the kitchen. In these pages though unlike my childhood, there is no animal flesh to be found. When my family and I became plant-based, it presented a cultural challenge as there were no plant-based meat free recipes for Nigerian food. I began to experience a culinary disconnect from my African/Nigerian ancestral roots. When I found Duchess Nena Ubani and her extensive knowledge of vegan Nigerian food, my whole world opened up once more and I reconnected again with African food which is culturally and emotionally important to me. In line with our shared interest, our friendship continues to grow.

I couldn't be more impressed and prouder of what this tenacious and creative lady has accomplished. My family and I cannot wait to start cooking with the recipes in this book, creating culinary and cultural memories for our children. Duchess Nena, well done and thank you.

by Victoria Koshoni

IGBO MAN AND HIS FOOD

Ndewo nu

Nutrition has become the cornerstone of maintaining good health. Different types of healthy dietary patterns are highly encouraged in order to foster good health, such as Mediterranean, paleo, vegan, etc. The Vegan diet plan or Veganism is not a popular diet plan in our society, but due to its beneficial attributes it is slowly gaining some attention. Interestingly, the Igbo people have a plant-based diet history, which is comparable to veganism but adopted a meat diet later on in their nutrition culture, as historical data shows they were originally plant-based eaters.

Igbo people are one of the largest ethnic groups in Africa. They can be found in the eastern part of Nigeria, Cameroon, and Equatorial Guinea. Igbo people were mainly farmers, and food is an important part of the Igbo culture. Food is culture and creates a sense of being. The Igbo people are generally known for different types of delicious soups, made from wild and domestically grown vegetables, spices, fermented foods, fruits, seeds and nuts. Their fundamental cuisine includes tuber vegetables such as cassava, yams, cocoyams, as well as legumes, grains amongst others.

The traditional Igbo food as within the truth of all cultures around the world, has been considerably influenced by way of their surrounding and history. Locally made dishes require unique processes and ingredients that offer a unique taste and texture. Some may be an acquired taste and others quite palate friendly. The recipes in this book are all of that and much more!

As we all know, variety is the spice of life and the same is true for nutrition. To gain major benefits from foods consumed, variety plays a huge role, the idea is simple, and it is the nutrients in foods that fuel the body, the more fuel the body is supported with the better mileage it would gain in terms of vitality and even longevity. *The Igbo Vegan* recipes offers variety and also an opportunity for all people in our society to be able to pursue and sustain a vegan lifestyle using locally grown produce.

These recipes offer affordability, accessibility and most importantly freshness, as they can all be locally sourced. Locally sourced foods offer much more nutrients. This book takes you on an Igbo culinary journey, and highlights the nutritive value of the numerous ingredients used in these recipes.

THE TRUTH ABOUT PALM OIL

I cannot write a book on Igbo veganism without talking about palm oil. This is because palm oil is a particularly important ingredient in Igbo cooking.

So what does this mean for an Igbo girl who just embraced veganism?

These and many other questions plagued me as I have eaten palm oil all my life and it was in all the food I loved growing up. This led to my research. Even though the actual plant is vegan, the use of palm oil is controversial amongst vegans with many striving to avoid it. Part of the controversy revolves around deforestation and the displacement of orangutans in South Asia, leading to carbon pollution from all the burning down of the forest. Having said this, it is important to understand the following:

1. What is palm oil?

Palm oil is oil from oil plant fruit tree (Elaeis Guineensis). Two types of oil can be produced from the oil palm tree.

a. **Pressed/crude palm oil** that comes from the process of squeezing the fruit. This is commonly called red oil due to its red colour. The palm oil is used for Igbo cooking, and appears in a number of receipes in this book.

b. **Palm kernel oil** which comes from the process of crushing the kernel. This is the more commercialised type. In Igbo traditional medicine, all parts of the plant are used for treatment. The most common is treating burns and improving skin conditions.

2. Palm trees are local to Igboland.

There are usually palm oil farms rather than plantations. It is an uncommon practice in our culture to destroy the forest by burning it just to plant. Palm fruits usually fall off the trees and germinate where they fall.

IGBO FERMENTED FOODS

Fermented foods are a major part of Igbo diet and there are myriads of them with some serving as main course meals, some serving as beverages while others constitute very important food condiments. The fermented foods that serve as main meals and beverages tend to be derived from raw materials that are rich in carbohydrate and some of the notable ones include 'garri' which is made from cassava. Akamu, which is derived from maize, and 'kaikai' beer which is gotten from the palm tree. On the other hand, those that function as food condiments are usually derived from the fermentation of seeds that are rich in protein. Examples of such include 'ugba', which is produced from African oil bean, 'ogiri' which is gotten from fermented oil seeds. They are excellent sources of vitamins and proteins.

Fermentation is widely regarded as the oldest means of preserving food and is without a doubt quite beneficial, as it not only prevents food spoilage, but also ensures that food can be stored for a longer time period. It also increases the digestibility of the food while also adding extra flavour to it.

The process of fermentation is carried out by combining plant ingredients with fungi or bacteria. These microorganisms contain fermentation microbes which then cover the plant ingredient that is to be fermented. After the appropriate number of days has elapsed for fermentation to take place, the ingredient is then processed into the desired food.

A good example is seen in the production of 'akpu'. After the cassava is peeled, it is washed and soaked in water for a few days. Once soft, it is then pressed and kept in bags which are squeezed until the water is drained out. Once this process is complete, an appropriate quantity of the cassava grains are then scooped into a pot of boiling water and cooked, stirred until edible. A similar process is used to produce 'garri' except that once the soaked cassava is fermented, it is then ground and kept in sacks until the liquid drains out. The dry cassava grains are then 'fried' in a dry large hot pan. This can be eaten in several different forms.

The major reason why fermentation is popular in Africa is its ability to convert sugars and other carbohydrates from the plant ingredients into usable end products.

Some of the benefits of fermentation include:

1. It brings about the elimination of anti-nutrients while inducing the production of beneficial nutrients in fermented food. This is because it uses up food energy thereby creating an unfavorable atmosphere for microorganisms that are responsible for food spoilage.
2. It makes foods more edible by modifying certain chemical compounds found in them. Some plants contain poisonous chemical compounds that serve as raw material for several staple foods in Igbo homes and this would have made them harmful to eat. However, fermentation eliminates these compounds and makes such plants edible. A good example of such is cassava, which is why it is never eaten raw but can be processed into various edible forms.
3. Fermentation also increases the nutritional values of foods, which contributes either directly or indirectly to living a healthy life.
4. It also aids digestion by promoting better metabolic system.

TABLE OF CONTENTS

Foreword 5
Introduction 7
The Truth About Palm Oil 9
Igbo fermented Foods 10

HERBS & SPICES
Nchanwu 17
Uda 18
Ogiri 18
Achi 19
Uhiokirihio 20
Utazi 20
Uziza 21
Ehuru 21
Ugu 22
Osi Oji 23
Oha 25
Ogbono 26
Ughughoro Leaves 27
Ukpo 28
Ofor 29
Osu 30
Akanwa 30
Bitterkola 31
Mmimi 32
Icheku 32
Ochicha 33
Kola nut 33
Anara 34
Ogalu 35
Udor Akpu enyi 35
Inine 36
Okwuru 37
Nte oka 37
Ukpa 38
Ose 39
Onugbo 40
Egusi 42

SOUPS (OFE)
Ofe Owerri 44
Ofe Ogbono 46
Ofe Oha/Ora 48
Ofe Onugbo 50
Ofe Okwuru 52
Ofe Egusi 54
Ofe Nsala 56
Ofe Akwu 58
Ofe Okazi 60
Ofe Akwukwo Anara 62
Ofe Achara 64

YAM RECIPES
JI Agworoagwo (Vegetable YAM) 68
JI Eghere Eghe (Fried YAM) 70
JI Agbugbo 71
Ji Nmanu 72
Akpuruakpu JI (Yam Balls) 74
Nri Asuruasu (Pounded YAM) 76
Oto (Water Yam Dumpling) 78
Ji Mmiri Oku (Yam Pepper Soup) 80
JI Ahuruahu (Roasted YAM) 82
ACHICHA Ede (Cocoyam) 84
Ayaraya JI 86

RICE (OSIKAPA) RECIPES
Native Jollof Rice 90
Rice and Stew 92
Coconut Rice 94
Nigerian Fried Rice 96

BEANS (AGWA) RECIPES
Ukwa 101
Boiled Beans 102
Beans Pottage 104
Okpa (Bambara Bean Cake) 106
Moi Moi 108

CASSAVA RECIPES
Akpu (Cassava Fufu) 112
Abacha (African Salad) 114
Nkwobi (African Salad) 116
Garri (Cassava Flakes) 118
Boiled Cassava 119

MAIZE/CORN RECIPES
Nri Oka (Corn Moi Moi) 122
Oka Na Ube (Roasted And Boiled) 124
Akamu (African Custard) 126
Agidi 128

ABRIKA (PLANTAIN) RECIPES
- Abrika Agworo Agwo (Plantain Pottage) 130
- Ukpo Ogede (Plantain Moi Moi) 132
- Ogede (Roasted Plantain) 134
- Abrika Eghere Eghe (Plantain Chips) 136

OTHER IGBO DISHES
- Akpurakpu Egusi (Egusi Cake) 138
- Okwa/Ose Oji 139
- Ihe Ndori (Vegetable Sauce) 140

CONTEMPORARY DISHES
- Jollof Spaghetti 144
- Kokoro 145
- Yaaji 146
- Kuli Kuli (Groundnut Cake) 147
- Puff-Puff 148
- Shuku Shuku (Coconut Cookies) 149
- Vegan Meat Pie 150
- Chin Chin 152
- Vegan Mushroom Suya 154
- Indomie' Pepper Soup 155

MEDICINAL JUICES & TEAS
- Bitterleave Juice 157
- Ugu And Pineapple Juice 158
- Aju Mbaise 159
- Nchanwu (Scent Leave) Juice 160
- Bitter Kola Drink 161
- Tiger Nut Juice 162
- Palm Wine (Ngwo) 163
- Kai Kai 164
- Mmiri Ukwa 165
- Zobo Drink 166

HERBS & SPICES

IGBO COOKING HERBS AND SPICES

"What medicine is there for hunger?... Obviously that which appeases hunger. But food does this, hence it must contain medicine - (Hippocrates 460 – 377 BC "About Winds")

For Igbo people, food is not just for feeding hunger but also used for healing and curing illnesses. To heal different ailments, a combination of herbs is used. These herbs are either eaten raw, juiced or cooked in food. In the subsequent pages we list a few of these herbs and how you can use them in cooking.

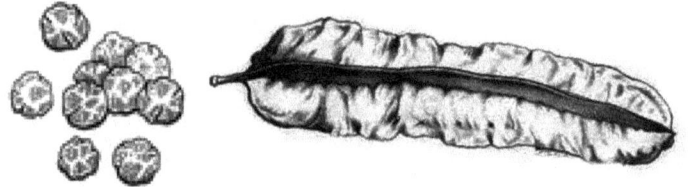

Nchanwu
(Ocimum Gratissimum)

Nchanwu, fondly called scent leaves because of its aromatic smell is a top herb used in Igbo traditional medicine because of its numerous benefits:

Benefits

Aids digestion

Used for oral hygiene

Used in treatment of mental illness

Used as a preservative

Treatment for fungal infection

Stem is used for chewing stick

Vaginal wash

Great for people with AIDS and HIV

Treatment of venereal disease

Treatment of cough and catarrh

Uda
(Grains of selim/Negro pepper)

Uda is a bitter and peppery spice, it is a major ingredient in cooking pepper soup, nkowbi and ofe nsala. It could be whole or in proper form. All parts of the uda (leaves, bark, fruits, seeds) are used for traditional medicine.

Benefits

Used to clear blood clot for new mothers

Encourages breast milk flow

Treatment for skin diseases

Treatment for malaria

Used as a contraceptive

Treatment respiratory of respiratory diseases

Regulates menstrual cycle

Induces labour

Laxative

Ogiri

Fermented seeds used for flavouring soups and African salads. Usually made out of castor oil, locust beans and egusi seeds. Ogiri has a pungent smell, but this can be reduced by freezing. Ogiri has many health benefits.

Benefits

Hypertension

Asthma

Arthritis

Diabetes

Epilepsy

Used as a contraceptive

Anti-inflammatory

Used in the making of local soups

Supports the immune

Antioxidant

Ingredients

(For ogiri receipe)

Prep/cooking time: 10 days 3 hours

1. 1 1/2 cups of egusi (melon seeds)
1. 10 banana leaves
2. Strings

Instructions

1. Wash the egusi with clean water, drain and set aside in a large bowl. Place a cooking pot over medium heat. Add about four cups of water and bring to boil. Once the water boils, pour into the bowl containing the egusi. Stir to combine and then sit for about one minute until soft. Drain and set aside.
2. Line a flat plate with the banana leaves, pour the egusi on the leaves, fold the leaves over the egusi (wrapping entirely) then tie with the strings. Place a cooking pot over medium heat, add in the wrapped egusi, and pour in enough water to cover. You can decide to place a rack

into the pot, place the wrap on the rack before pouring in water. This will prevent burning.

3. Cover the pot and cook for about 3 hours until the water dries up. Once the time elapses, use a spatula to press out any remaining water from the wrap, then let to cool for a few minutes. Place the egusi wrap back into the pot, cover and place in a kitchen cabinet and let sit for 4 days.
4. Unwrap the egusi, pour the seeds into a mortar and pound till smooth then set aside. Line a medium mixing bowl with more banana leaves, pour the smooth paste into it, cover with another banana leave then cover the entire bowl with a plastic wrap. Place the bowl in a kitchen cabinet and let sit for another 4-6 days.
Stir and use as desired.

Note
Castor seeds can be used as a substitute for melon seeds (egusi). Egusi seeds are mostly used in Nigeria because of it's availability.

Achi
(Brachystegia Eurycoma)

It is used as a thickener for cooking soups.

Benefits

Anti-inflammatory

Analgesic

Antioxidant

Lowers blood sugar

Anti-cancer

Anti-microbial

Promotes bowel movement

Lowers cholesterol

High in vitamins

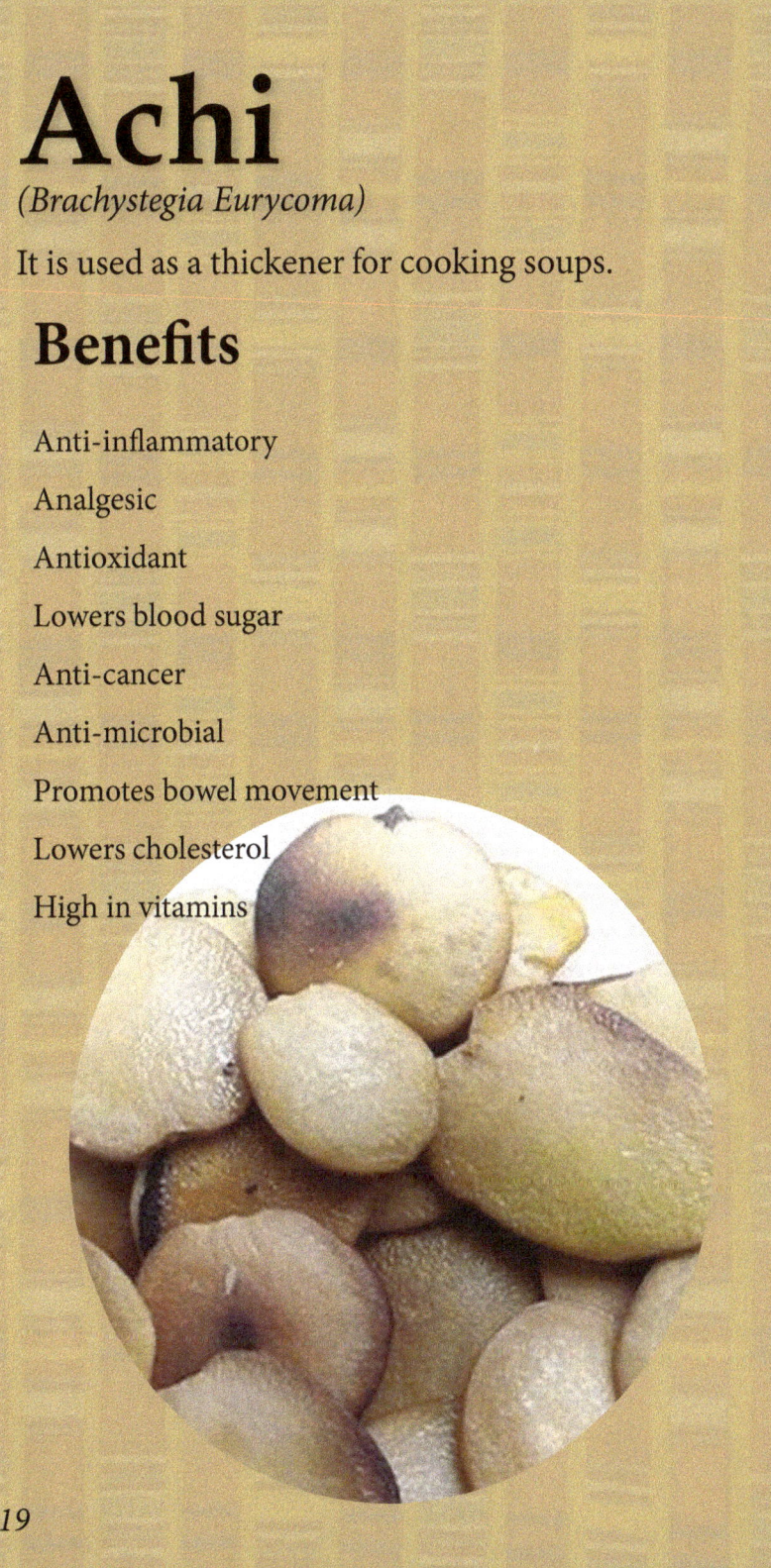

Uhiokirihio
(Aridan fruit)

Benefits

Used for making essential oils

Treats arthritis/ rheumatism

Treats diabetes

Lowers cholesterol

Insect repellent

Diuretic

Anti-sticking

Relieves headaches

Utazi
(Gongronena Latifolium)

Utazi is a plant farmed for its bitter sweet leaves. It can be eaten raw or cooked in soups/sauces.

Benefits

Anti-inflammatory used as an analgesic

Antioxidant

Antibacterial

Boosts fertility

Anti-sticking

Laxative

Antifungal

Reduces blood pressure

Reduces blood sugar

Treatment of tumours

Anti-asthmatic

Uziza
(Piper Guineense)

Uziza is used in two forms: Akwukwo uziza (uziza leaf) and mkpuro uziza (uziza seeds/pepper).

Benefits

Treatment of fertility in both men and women

Aphrodisiac

Anti-inflammatory

Anti-cancer

Insecticides

Leprosy treatment

Treatment of intestinal disorders

Postnatal cleanser

Antioxidant

Ehuru
(Monodora Myrisitica)

Ehuru is also known as African nutmeg because of its smell and taste similar to a nutmeg. Its aroma and taste makes it a favourite for making African salad. The shell is broken and meat insides used.

Benefits

Used for making Essential oils

Treating arthritis/rheumatism

Treatment of diabetes

Lowers cholesterol

Insect repellent

Diuretic

Anti-sticking

Relieves headaches

Ugu

(Fluted pumpkin leaves)

Telfairia occidentalis is a tropical vine grown in West Africa. This leaf is usually used in majority of Igbo dishes. It can also be juiced.

Benefits

Anti-diabetic

Rich in antioxidants

Maintains the body tissue

High in fibre

Treating hormonal imbalance

Anti-convulsion

Iron boost and anaemia prevention

High in potassium and magnesium

Effective for weight loss

Promotes fertility due to dietary fibre

Can improve memory (Vitamin and magnesium)

Ose Oji
(Alligator Pepper)

This is usually offered to special guests alongside garden eggs and kolanut. Can be used as garnish for African salad, pepper soup and local stew. It is usually sold in pods and the seeds picked out. It can also be eaten raw.

Benefits

Treatment of indigestion, asthma and dysentery

Antioxidant

Postpartum bleeding

Aphrodisiac

Wound healing

Disinfectant

Anti-inflammatory

Anti- malarial

Analgesic

Treatment of skin-diseases

Lowers blood sugar

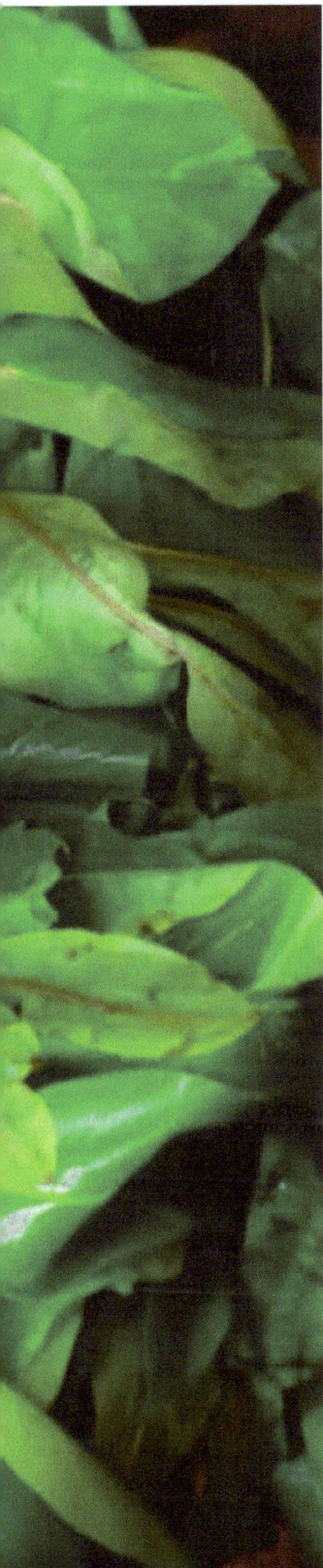

Oha
(Pterocarpus mildraedii)

Oha's health benefit is often overlooked due to the delicate nature of its leaves. These leaves fall into the category of super foods as they are high in dietary fibre that improves the digestive function and encourages absorption of nutrients by the body. In addition to this, the following are the benefits of this awesome plant:

Benefits

It regulates the blood glucose levels.

Great for gut health

High in antioxidant

High in iron

Good for bone health

Used in the treatment of some cancers.

Energy booster, especially for athletes

Helps maintain the body's alkaline level.

Ogbono
(Irvingia gabonensis)

Ogbono is a soup thickener and usually slimy when cooked. It is commonly called wild mango because it bears fruit similar to mango. Ogbono seeds are used for cooking and making herbal medicine. The fruit can also be eaten raw.

Benefits

Lowers cholesterol due to high fibre content

Breaks down fat in the body

For treatment of diabetes as it lowers blood sugar

Aids weight loss

Ughughoro Leaves/ Gourd
(Curcubita maxima)

It is a highly nutritious leaf used for making soups and pottages. It is juiced for the treatment of some ailments

Benefits

Fights against cancer
Increases fertility in women
Lowers cholesterol
Treatment of infections and convulsion
Treatment of diabetes
Blood Boosterbooster
Boost Boosts the immune system
Treatment of HIV

Ukpo comes in pods containing up to 3 seeds. This is a soup thickener. It is usually cracked, boiled and diluted. It can also be boiled and spiced then eaten as a snack.

Benefits

High in protein

Treatment of urinary tract infection

Treatment neurological and menstruation disorders

Treatment of Parkinson's disease

Constipation

Ukpo
(Detarium microcapum)

Ofor
(Detarium microcapum)

This is used as a soup thickener

Benefits

Diuretic

Anti-inflammatory

Lowers blood glucose

Osu
(Pleurotus tuberregium)

Osu is generally used as a soup thickener. It is an edible fungus-mushroom commonly called King Tuber mushroom. It is a tropical sclerotia mushroom.

Benefits

Antioxidant

Anti-inflammatory

Protects the liver

Antipathogenic

Antimitogenic

Lowers fat levels in the blood – hypolipidemic

Used to treat headache, fever, chest pain, persistent cough, and heart disease

Lowers blood sugar and cholesterol

Treatment of digestive issues

Boosts immune system

This is a type of salt. It is used in the cooking of African salad and ugba. It is important to take in small quantities as it can increase blood pressure, block absorption of protein, lower sperm count, affect liver and kidney, induce labour, or terminate pregnancy.

Benefits

It acts as a preservative

Used in making herbal medicine and concoctions

Relief from constipation

Aids lactation

Anti-fungal

A tenderiser for cooking beans and ukwa. Reduces cooking time

Treatment of cough/ expectorant

Akanwa
(Kaun/Potash)

Aki Ilu

(Bitterkola/Garcinia kola)

It is a nut/seed usually presented to welcome guests. Often chewed raw as a snack. Bitter but with a sweet after taste.

Benefits

Fights glaucoma

Anti-malarial

Treatment of STDs

Boosts immune system

Improves lung function

Relieves symptoms of osteoarthritis

Increases sex drive

Anti-parasitic

Treatment of colds

Weight loss

Anti-cellulite

Mmimi
(Pepper fruit /*Dennettia tripetala*)

It can be eaten raw as a snack or used as a peppery spice for seasoning soups and stews. It is also offered to guests alongside garden eggs, kolanut and ose oji.

They come in three colours: green, red and orange. Green is spicy and red is sweet. All parts are used for medicine - leaves, roots, barks, and fruits.

Benefits

Anti-inflammatory

Anti-viral

Treatment of nausea and vomiting

Treatment of ulcers

Treatment of stomach upset

Anti-microbial

Antibacterial

Treatment of convulsion

For postpartum treatment used in pepper soup

Treatment of cough

Prevention of prostate cancer

Controls blood sugar levels

Icheku
(Black tamirid/ *dialium guineense*)

Its fruit can be eaten raw or juiced. The leaves can also be eaten raw

Benefits

For the treatment of:
Bronchitis
Toothache
Astringent
Diuretic

Ochicha
(Bush kola/ monkey kola)

It has an edible yellow or white flesh with a brown coat. Ochicha leaves are usually used as herbs for treating eye infections.

Benefits

Good source of calcium, phosphorus, iron, sodium, zinc, and potassium

Vitamins A and B2 for eye health

Increases metabolism

Aids in production of red blood cells

Energy boost.

Antioxidant

Kola Nut
(Kola nut/Cola nitida)

Benefits

Used to flavour sodas

Increases energy

Boosts metabolism

Aids digestion

Anti-bacterial

Treatment of headaches

Treatment of asthma

Stimulant

Cola Nitida is usually eaten raw. Kola or kola nut is revered by Igbo people. There is a popular saying in Igboland; "He who brings kola, brings life." It is usually presented at special occasians and is blessed by an elder or titled man before being shared. Only men are allowed to climb a kola tree as it is associated with men. Use sparingly as it may increase blood pressure or cause stomach upset.

Anara
(Garden eggs/*solanum aethiopicum*)

Used in the same way you would an eggplant. Gre[at]
for making sauces or eaten raw.

Benefits

Promotes Weight Loss

Rich in antioxidants

Rich in vitamin B

Promotes healthy bone

Aids digestion

Prevents anaemia

Prevents diabetes

Maintains blood pressure levels

Prevents heart diseases

Ogalu
(Senna alata)

This is also known as ring candle plant. The leaves are juiced for use.

Benefits

Antibacterial

Antifungal

Anti-inflammatory

Anti-cancer

Analgesic and laxative

Also used for treatment of skin infections.

Treatment of hypertension

Udor Akpu Enyi
(Tinospora cordifolia)

All parts of this plant are used in traditional Igbo medicine, but the bark is an important ingredient in the making of the famous 'Aju Mbaise.'

Benefits

Anti-viral

Antidote for snake bite and scorpion sting

Treatment of leprosy, diarrhoea, and dysentery.

Improves fertility

Treatment of some cancers and jaundice

Inine

(Amaranth green/*amaranthus viridis l*)

Used for making soups and stews

Benefits

High fibre

Cholesterol control

High in iron

For maintaining eye health

Antioxidant

Brain health

Regulates blood pressure

High in vitamins A, C, K, B6

High in potassium

Okwuru
(Okra/_Abelmoschus esculentus_**)**

Okra is a nutritious food with many health benefits. In Igboland, Okra can be eaten raw

Benefits

Rich in magnesium, folate, fibre, antioxidants, and vitamins C, K1, and A.

Heart health

Blood sugar control.

Anti-cancer

Natural relaxant

Aphrodisiac

Nte oka
(Water leaf/ _talinum fruticosum_)

Nte oka(waterleaf) earned its name due to its high water content.

Benefits

Supports bone health

Supports eye health

Treatment of iron deficiency and anemia

Reduces the risk of developing Alzheimer's disease and slows age-related cognitive decline.

Ukpa
(Tetracarpidium conophorum)

Ukpa is a fruit and herb that is found in the shell of a nut. This is a well sought after herb nut used for medicine. The seed is roasted and the soft fruit inside eaten as a snack or used as a thickener for soup.

Benefits

Treatment of insomnia

Lowers cholesterol

Prevention of cancer

Anti-inflammatory properties

Anti-ageing

Regulates menstrua flow

Boosts cognitive functions

Prevents miscarriages in pregnant women

Treatment for infertility

Prevention of cardiovascular diseases

Aphrodisiac

Treatment of headaches

Antidote to poison

Treatment of malaria

Promotes healthy immune systems

Ose
(Pepper/Capsicum chinense)

Benefits

Anti inflammation

Natural pain relief

Heart benefits

Clear congestion

Boost immunity

Help stop the spread of prostate cancer

Prevent stomach ulcers

Weight loss

Lowers risk of type 2 diabetes

Rich source of vitamin C

Onugbo
(Bitterleaf / *Vernona amygdalina*)

This is a very underrated leaf due to its bitterness. It is a healer plant with many health benefits. It is commonly known as bitterleaf. It is usually washed and the bitter water extracted to make the leaves more palatable. It is used in the making of the famous bitterleaf soup.

Benefits

High in vitamins

Antifungal

Anti-carcinogenic

Antibacterial

Treatment of diabetes

Treatment of sexually transmitted diseases

Anti-helminthic

Boosts immune system

Boost fertility

Encourages lactation

Detoxifier

Treats insomnia

Natural insect repellent

Treatment of hepatitis b and c

Worm expellant/anti-parasitic

Strengthening muscles and bones

Balances oestrogen levels

Egusi is usually used for cooking soups, stews, making of ogiri or for making akpuruakpu egusi (Egusi cake). Egusi oil can also be extracted for use in cooking.

Benefits

Anti-inflammatory properties

Helps fight cancer

Anti-arthritic

Great for skin

Aids digestion

Boosts appetite

Egusi
(Cucumeropsis mannii)

SOUPS (OFE)

OFE OWERRI
(Owerri Soup)

Ofe Owerri is super healthy and incredibly delicious. This soup is famously known as the Owerri people's national soup. Owerri is the state capital of Imo State, one of the 5 eastern states in Nigeria. The major ingredient in this soup is cocoyam. One cup of cocoyam offers about 6.7 grams of fibre, 30% manganese (DV), 22% of vitamin B-6 (DV), 19% vitamin E.

Ingredients

1. 5 medium-sized cocoyams
2. 1 cup of dried Ukazi leaves
3. 2 handfuls of fluted pumpkin leaves
4. 2 stock cubes or as your taste may require.
5. 2 wraps of ogiri,
6. 3 Scotch Bonnets or dried pepper as an alternative
7. Salt to taste
8. 2 table spoons of palm oil
9. 4 cups of water.

Instructions

1. Wash the cocoyam thoroughly and immerse in a water filled pot. Cook the cocoyam for about 30 minutes or until soft. Remove from heat and leave to cool a bit. Peel off and discard the skin, mash with a mortar or blender until it becomes smooth and set aside.
2. Using clean water, wash the leafy vegetables separately and slice into small pieces with a knife and keep aside.
3. Place a large cooking pot over medium heat and add the cups of water. Add other ingredients like pepper, stock cubes, and salt to taste.
4. Once the water stock from (3) above is boiled, add other ingredients like the palm oil, and ogiri. Stir the mixture and boil again over high heat until the ogiri starts to flavour.
5. Add the mashed cocoyam in portions with the aid of a spoon and boil again for another twenty minutes until the cocoyam starts to melt and becomes creamy in nature.
6. Once the thick paste is formed, stir the soup properly, add the sliced leaves and stir again. Taste for pepper and salt and add more if needed. Simmer over low heat for five minutes.
7. Once ready, serve with pounded yam or fufu and enjoy.

NUTRITIONAL CONTENT:
Calories 332, total fat 7g, carbohydrates 20g, and protein 18g.

OFE OGBONO
(Ogbono Soup)

The major ingredient in this soup is ogbono, also known as Wild Mango. Aside from being 100% organic it contains some amazing nutrients such as protein (multiple amino acids), calcium, and magnesium. Potassium, sodium, phosphorous and iron among other nutrients. The soup, especially with fluted pumpkin offers multiple B-complex vitamins such as folate (Vitamin–B9), Vitamin-B2, etc. It is also beneficial for diabetics.

Ingredients

1. 1 cup of ground ogbono seeds.
2. 4 table spoons of red palm oil.
3. 1 cup or more of frozen spinach, fluted pumpkin (ugu) or bitter leaves as vegetables.
4. 4 habanero (yellow) or scotch bonnet peppers to taste
5. 1 small onion
6. 2 stock seasoning cubes
7. Salt to taste

Instructions

1. Wash the vegetables with clean water and cut them with a knife and keep aside.
2. Using a medium-sized cooking pot, pour in the palm oil.
3. Once the palm oil is melted (palm oil may become solid under room temperature) turn off the heat and add the the ground ogbono.
4. Use a cooking spoon or a spatula to dissolve the ogbono in the palm oil.
5. Once the ground ogbono is well combined, place back on low heat. Stir periodically until the ogbono starts to thicken and draw.
6. Add a little amount of hot water to the ogbono along with pepper and salt to taste. Keep stirring until all the water is absorbed.
7. Place the cut vegetables into the soup. Stir appropriately, and let the soup stand. Cover over low heat for 8 minutes while stirring every two to three minutes to prevent it from sticking to the bottom of the pot. If the ogbono is too thick, add more water and keep cooking until the soup is properly cooked.
8. Serve the soup with pounded yam or any fufu of choice.

NUTRITIONAL CONTENTS:
Calories 270.0, total fat 3.0 g, total carbohydratetotal 8.0 g, and protein 15.0 g.

OFE OHA/ORA
(Oha/Ora Soup)

Oha (or ora) are the leaves used in this soup. They are the major ingredient. Oha leaves are super healthy and contain multiple nutrients such as calcium, multiple amino acids (protein), iron, potassium, fibre, vitamins-A and C, etc. Green leafy vegetables are best consumed freshly cooked as reheating releases carcinogenic substance.

Ingredients

1. 120 grams of oha leaves properly shredded with clean hands and washed with clean water
2. 7 pieces of sliced uziza leaves.
3. 6 cups of water or as required for preferred consistency
4. 1 table spoon of Cameroon pepper,
5. 1 teaspoon coarsely blended yellow scotch bonnet or habanero pepper
6. 1 tablespoon of ogiri
7. 2 tablespoons of cocoyam paste for thickening
10. 3 Seasoning cubes

Instructions

1. In a cooking pot, add the cups of water, pepper, seasoning cubes, salt, and palm oil. Stir the mixture appropriately and boil over medium heat for about 15 minutes.
2. Add a little amount of hot water to the ogiri and dissolve with a spoon. Add the dissolved ogiri into the cooking pot. Take out a little amount of the boiling soup sauce and add to the cocoyam paste, mix properly and place it back into the cooking pot. Add more seasonings if needed.
3. Once the soup starts boiling, it thickens. Add in the oha and uziza leaves and let it stand for about 5 minutes.
4. Serve with any fufu of choice or pounded yam.

NUTRITIONAL CONTENTS:
Calories 350, total fat 5g, carbohydrates 18g, and

OFE ONUGBO
(Bitter Leaf Soup)

Ofe onugbo is a healthy soup. It is made with cocoyam and bitter leaves amongst other amazing ingredients. Bitter leaf's bitter taste makes it distinct from other vegetables. The leaves help in the reduction of high blood sugar levels, which makes it great for diabetics. It also helps to detox the body, and it is good for mild stomach ailments. However, high intake may not be great for women trying to conceive or in their first trimester due to the possibility of a miscarriage.

Bitter leaf contains vitamins-A, C, B-1, B 2; fiber; manganese, zinc, iron, calcium, potassium, etc. Cocoyam used in this soup has much better nutritional quality than other root and tuber crops. However, it is a high glycemic food, thus not so great for diabetes, but the mixture of bitter leaf balances out the effects once used in moderate quantities.

Ingredients

1. 1 cup washed and squeezed bitter leaf to remove much of the bitter taste
2. 6 small tubers of cocoyam boiled and made into a smooth paste
3. 4 tablespoons of red palm oil
4. 3 stock cubes
5. 1 teaspoon of ogiri (fermented seasoning)
6. Some cups of water as required

Instructions

1. Ensure the leaves are properly cleaned with no impurities. Wash out most of the bitterness, but leave some to give the soup the necessary bitter hint, and keep aside for later.
2. Wash the cocoyam thoroughly in water with the skin on and place into another cooking pot. Add water to the level of the cocoyams in the pot, and boil over medium heat for about 20 minutes or until the cocoyam is well cooked and soft to touch.
3. Once the cocoyam is cooked, remove from heat and leave to cool for a bit. Peel off the skin and mash with a mortar or blender until it becomes smooth and keep aside.
4. Place a large cooking pot over medium heat and add water to it. Add ingredients like pepper, stock cubes, and salt to taste.
5. Once the water stock from (4) above is boiled, add other ingredients like the palm oil, and ogiri. Stir the mixture and boil again over high

heat until the ogiri starts to flavor.
6. Add in the mashed cocoyam in portions with the aid of a spoon and boil again for a few minutes until the cocoyam dissolves and the soup thickens. Stir the soup properly, add the washed bitter leaves and stir again. Taste for pepper and salt and add more if needed. Simmer over low heat for 5 minutes.
7. Once ready, serve with pounded yam or fufu. Enjoy.

NUTRITIONAL CONTENTS
Calories 417, sodium 160mg, total fat 23g, potassium 503mg, saturated fat 8g, total carbohydrates 15g, dietary fibre 2g, sugars 0g, protein 37g and cholesterol 76mg.

OFE OKWURU
(Okra Soup)

As highly accessible and available as okra vegetable is, so is its nutrients. Okra is an incredible source of folate, vitamins –c, k1, A, fibre and antioxidants. Okra supports healthy pregnancy due to its folate content, heart health, and promotes blood sugar control. It is also said to have anti-cancer properties.

Ingredients

1. 2 cups of chopped okra
2. 3 tablespoons of red palm oil
3. Pepper and salt to taste
4. 1 small onion bulb (optional)
5. 1 cup sliced pumpkin leaves/fresh or frozen spinach as vegetables
6. 2 stock or bouillon cubes.
7. Water as required.

Instructions

1. Wash the okra with clean water and cut them into tiny pieces by making horizontal cuts from the pointed tip followed by vertical cuts and then slicing it accordingly.
2. Wash the desired vegetable and cut into smaller pieces.
3. Place a large cooking pot over medium heat and add water to it. Add ingredients like onions and stock cubes, pepper and salt to taste and boil over medium heat for about 10 minutes.
4. In another cooking pot, pour the palm oil and heat over medium heat; once the oil is hot, add the sliced okra and stir. Add the water stock little by little, and keep stirring the okra until it starts to draw.
5. Add the rest of the water stock and stir properly. Then, add your desired vegetable, and more pepper and salt to taste if needed. Stir properly.
6. Cover the cooking pot and let the okro soup simmer for about 2 minutes then serve with your desired fufu.

NUTRITIONAL CONTENTS:
Calories 92.4, Total total fat 3.2 g, cholesterol 34.6 mg, sodium 685.8 mg, potassium 265.2 mg, total carbohydrate 6.0 g, dietary fibre 2.6 g, sugars 2.0 g, and protein 10.9 g.

OFE EGUSI
(Egusi Soup)

Egusi is a popular Nigeria dish, the main ingredient is the melon seed powder known as egusi. Egusi is healthy and rich in multiple nutrients such as vitamins -B1, B2, B6, B9, protain, manganese, magnesium, zinc, iron, copper, etc. However, it is rich in omega -6 fatty acids, which must be consumed in moderation. Since egusi is high in fat it is best cooked with little palm oil.

Ingredients

1. 2 cups of ground egusi (melon) seeds.
2. 4 tablespoons of red palm oil (or as desired).
3. 2 tablespoonof mixed peppers(long capsicum & habanero)
4. 1 tablespoon onion paste
5. Salt as required
6. 2 vegetable stock cubes of choice.
7. 1 teaspoon onion paste
8. 2 tablespoon chopped onions
9. 2 cups fluted pumpkin leaves; spinach or 1 cup bitter leaves or a mixture of all if desired (if you choose all 3 vegetables use a total quantity of 2 cups)
10. I teaspoon dry okpehe or any locust bean seasoning.
11. 8 cups of water or as desired to meet preferred consistency.

Instructions

1. In a large cooking pot, add 4 teaspoons of palm oil.
2. After the oil is hot, add chopped onions. allow onions to cook until soft
3. Add warm water into the egusi and make a runny paste.
4. After 5-8 minutes of cooking onions in oil add the egusi paste and stir intermittently.
5. Add seasoning cubes, pepper and onions paste, add water and boil over medium heat.
6. Once it is properly boiled for about 40 minutes, add the locust bean and let it cook for a few minutes (3-5). Finally add vegetable(s) of choice. If it is bitter, allow to simmer a while longer than ugwu, for about 3 minutes.
7. Once the soup is ready, serve with your favourite fufu meal.

NUTRITIONAL CONTENTS
Calories 462, Sodium 1,815mg, total fat 28g, saturated oil 6g, total carbohydrates 13g, dietary fibre 4g, sugars 4g, protein 43g and cholesterol 93mg.

OFE NSALA
(Nsala Soup)

Herbs are amazing. They serve as medicine and food. Utazi contains incredible beneficial properties. It is known to have anti-bacterial and anti-inflammatory properties, boosts fertility and appetite, helps prevents constipation by promoting good digestion, alleviates cough symptoms and much more. It is rich in antioxidants, multiple vitamins and minerals and healthy oils.

Ingredients

1. 2 cups of fresh or 1 cup of dry Utazi Leaves
2. 2 cups of white yam paste
3. I teaspoon ground uziza seeds
4. 1 tablespoon habanero peppers (red and yellow)
5. Salt to taste
6. 2 stock cubes of choice
7. 1 teaspoon ogiri (traditional fermented seasoning)
8. Water as required

Instructions

1. Wash yam thoroughly and then peel the brown skin off the yam, then wash with clean water and slice the yam into smaller pieces. Boil the yam over medium heat for about 20 minutes. Once the yams are ready, pound in a mortar or blend with a high-speed blender or a food processor and keep aside.
2. Place a big enough cooking pot over medium heat, and add water to it. Add ingredients like the stock cubes, pepper and salt to taste and boil over medium heat for about 5 minutes. Add the ogiri and then the mashed white yam in portions with the aid of a spoon and boil again for another 5 minutes until the yam is properly dissolved and has a thick consistency.
3. Add the uziza leaves and a little water and simmer for 2-5 minutes.
4. Serve with desired fufu.

NUTRITIONAL CONTENTS
Calories 254, 9%, total fat 5.7g, 13%, saturated fat 2.5g, 18%, cholesterol 55mg. 11%. sodium 263mg 10%, total carbohydrates 28.6g, 16% dietary fibre 4.1g, sugars 0.5g, and protein 21g.

OFE AKWU
(Palm fruit Soup)

Ofe Akwu is a tasty delicacy, but not as nutrients dense as most of the other listed soups. Because of the high oil content. It is best consumed occasionally.

Ingredients

1. 1 kg of palm fruits or 500 grams of tinned palm fruit concentrate
2. ½ cup scent leaves (nchuanwu)
3. 1 medium onion
4. Salt to taste
5. 1 tablespoon yellow habanero pepper paste
6. 1 teaspoon ogiri (fermented traditional seasoning)
7. 1 or 2 stock cubes

Instructions

1. In a large cooking pot, wash and boil the palm fruits over medium heat for about 20 minutes or until they become tender when bitten.
2. Once the palm fruits are cooked, pound in the mortar and extract the palm fruit concentrate using hot water. You can use tinned palm fruits concentrate as alternative.
3. Wash the Scent Leaves with clean water and slice into small pieces.
4. Pour the extracted palm fruit concentrate into a sizeable cooking pot, and boil until the concentrate becomes thick as desired and red oil appears on the surface.
5. Add the rest of the ingredients like onions, pepper, and salt for taste, and cook for ten minutes, so the ingredients will integrate.
6. Add sliced scent leaves and simmer for about 2 minutes. Once cooked, serve with any grain or pseudo grain of choice such as rice quinoa, fonio, Acha) etc.

NUTRITIONAL CONTENTS:
Calories 265.4, total fat 28.3g, saturated fat 13.9g, cholesterol 7.2mg, sodium 11.6 mg, potassium 193.3mg, total carbohydrate 2.9g, dietary fiber 0.8g, sugars 1.1g, and protein 1.6g.

OFE OKAZI
(Okazi Soup)

Okazi leaves offer great culinary value. The leaves are also a good source of protein. It has been noted as anti-inflammatory, anti-carcinogenic and is rich in antioxidants.

Ingredients

1. 2 cups of sliced okazi
2. 1 teaspoon of dry pepper powder
3. 1 tablespoon of achi or ofor powder for thickening
4. 1 tablespoon of uziza leaves
5. 2 tablespoons of ogiri paste
6. 1 teaspoon yellow/red habanero pepper.
7. 2 tablespoons of palm oil.
8. 1 vegan bouillon (optional.)
9. Salt as to taste
10. 1 stock cube.

Instructions

1. Place the ogiri, habanero pepper and sliced uziza leaves in a mortar and mash together. Place the mashed ingredients in a plate and set aside.
2. Place a pot over medium heat and add water to it. Add stock cubes, pepper powder, vegan bouillon, and salt to taste, and boil over medium heat for about 10 minutes.
3. Once the water stock is boiled, add some of the achi powder and cook for 10 minutes until the water thickens.
4. Add the mashed ingredients and palm oil and simmer for about 5 minutes or until the palm oil is totally mixed with the water stock.
5. Add achi or ofo (as desired), wash, slice and add the okazi leaves, and cook for about 10 additional minutes. Taste for seasonings and add more if needed.
6. Serve with any desired fufu.

NUTRITIONAL CONTENTS:
calories 265.4, total fat 28.3g, saturated fat 13.9g, cholesterol 7.2mg, sodium 11.6 mg, potassium 193.3mg, total car-bohydrate 2.9g, dietary fibre 0.8g, sugars 1.1g, and protein 1.6g.

OFE AKWUKWO ANARA
(Garden Egg Leaf Soup)

The major ingredient in this soup is garden egg leaves. Garden egg leaves offer great culinary value. They are rich in phenolic, a compound that acts as an antioxidant. Garden egg leaves are rich in fibre, copper, manganese, vitamins -B6, and B1, amongst others. As with all leafy vegetables, it is best consumed when freshly cooked, as reheating hinders benefits due to nitrosamines formation in the course of reheating most vegetables.

Ingredients

1. 1 medium finely chopped onion.
2. 2 seasoning cubes.
3. 1 teaspoon of ogiri (fermented seasoning)
4. 1 teaspoon habanero pepper paste or as desired
5. 3 tablespoons of palm oil
6. 2 tablespoons of achi or cocoyam as thickeners
7. 2 cups garden egg leaves, or as desired
8. 2 cups of water

Instructions

1. Wash the garden egg leaves and slice into smaller pieces and set aside.
2. Place a large cooking pot over medium heat and add water to it. Add ingredients (chopped onion, seasoning cubes, salt) allow it to cook for about 8 minutes.
3. Add ogiri, the rest of the seasoning cubes, and palm oil, cook for 5 minutes, then add your preferred thickener (i.e. achi or cocoyam) and cook until it dissolves completely.
4. Add more water to the soup, taste for salt and pepper and add more if needed.
5. Add the sliced leaves to the soup and simmer for 1 minute.
6. Serve with fufu of choice.

NUTRITIONAL CONTENTS:
Calories 264.2, total fat 22.0g, cholesterol 178.6mg, sodium 334.5mg, Potassium 409.3 mg, total carbohydrate 6.6g, dietary fibre 1.5g, sugars 3.5g and protein 11.5g.

OFE ACHARA
(Elephant Grass Soup)

The main ingredients in this soup are achara and egusi. This delicacy is famous amongst Isiala Ngwa and Umuahia people of Abia State. Achara comes from the mature shoots of the edible elephant grass. It has great nutritional value, being rich in multiple amino acids, fibre, phosphorous, potassium, selenium, carotene, calcium, zinc, vitamin – B6, amongst others.

Ingredients

1. 1 medium bunch of Achara
2. 20 small balls of mgbam (egusi balls)
3. 2 tablespoons of ground achi
4. 1½ tablespoon of dried and ground pepper
5. 3 table spoons of palm oil
6. 2 stock cubes of choice
7. 6 cups of water
8. Salt to taste

Instructions

1. Slowly rip off the external layers of the achara, cut what is left into smaller pieces and set aside.
2. Prepare egusi balls and also set aside.
3. Place a large cooking pot over medium heat and add water in it. Add other ingredients: salt, stock cubes and chopped onion. Let it simmer.
4. Add the egusi balls into the water stock. Cook for about 30 minutes.
5. Add the palm oil, ground pepper, and the sliced achara to the water stock and stir properly. Allow to cook for 5 minutes.
6. Add a small amount of cold water to the achi and mix to form a paste. Add the achi paste into the soup and cook for another 5 minutes until the desired thickness is achieved. Taste the soup for pepper and salt and add more if needed.
7. Serve with any fufu of choice.

NUTRITIONAL CONTENTS:
Calories 209, total fat 7g, carbohydrates 20g, and protein 18g.

YAM RECIPES

There are different types of yams in Igbo cuisine such as white yam, bitter yam, water yam, etc. There are also other tuber vegetables that are grouped in the yams category such as sweet potato, Irish potato, etc.

Tubers are generally a good source of energy rich carbohydrate and soluble dietary fibre. Dietary fibre helps reduce constipation, decreases bad (LDL) cholesterol levels by binding to it in the intestines, and lowers colon cancer risk by preventing toxic compounds in the food from adhering to the colon mucosa. Tubers are also an excellent source of B-complex group of vitamins. They provide adequate daily requirements of pyridoxine (vitamin B6), thiamin (vitamin B1), riboflavin (vitamin-B2), folates (vitamin-B9), pantothenic acid (vitamin B5) acid and niacin (vitamin B3). These vitamins mediate various metabolic functions in the body.

Most tuber vegetables, especially yams and sweet potatoes contain a good amount of minerals such as copper, calcium, potassium, iron, manganese, and phosphorus amongst other nutrients.

JI AGWOROAGWO
(Vegetable Yam)

Ingredients

1. 4 cups of medium size cubed yams
2. 3 tablespoons of red palm oil.
3. 1 stock cube
4. 4 habanero peppers
5. 1 big sized onion.
6. 2 stock cubes and salt as desired
7. 5 cups amaranth greens
8. 3 cups of water

Instructions

1. Peel the yam in cold water to keep it from oxidising as some yams do turn reddish if this process is not followed keep. Keep yam aside.
2. Using a blender, food processor or grinding stone, blend other peppers and half of the onion until fine.
3. In a medium sized cooking pot, add palm oil and heat over medium heat. Add the pepper and onion paste to the hot oil, and sauté for a few minutes.
4. Combine the yam, stock cubes, salt, and stir. Pour in some water (2 cups or as required). Cook over medium heat for about 15 minutes (with the lid on) or until the yam becomes fairly soft.
5. While the yam is cooking, clean the amaranth greens and slice thinly. Keep aside.
6. Once the yam is cooked, taste for seasonings and add more if needed. Finally, add the chopped amaranth greens and mix. Remove the yam from heat and serve.

NUTRITIONAL CONTENTS:
Calories 155.6, total fat 3.5g, cholesterol 4.7mg, sodium 125.4mg, potassium 742.8mg, total carbohydrate 28.8g, dietary fibre 5.4g, sugars 0.3g and protein 4.1g.

JI EGHERE EGHE
(Fried Yam)

Ingredients

1. One small tuber of white yam
2. Vegetable oil
3. Salt to taste

Instructions

1. Peel off the skin of the yam and cut it into any shape of choice. Wash the sliced yam in clean water and place in a medium bowl. Add a little salt for taste and toss evenly to combine.
2. Add vegetable oil in a deep-frying pan over medium heat. Once the oil is hot, add the yam in batches and fry for about 10-15 minutes until it turns golden brown or lighter. Repeat the same process with the rest of the yam. Once the yam is fried, place them on paper towels to drain excess oil.
3. Serve with any sauce of choice.

NUTRITIONAL CONTENTS: Calories 451.9, total fat 40.6g, cholesterol 0.0mg, sodium 1,358.2mg, potassium 455.8mg, total carbohydrate 22.8g, dietary fibre 2.7g, sugars 4.3g and protein 1.0g.

JI AGBUGBO
(Mixed Yam & Oil Bean)

Ingredients

1. A few cups of sliced yam or as much as is required.
2. Salt and pepper to taste
3. Utazi leaves or garden egg leaves alternatively
4. 3 teaspoons of palm oil
5. Ukpaka (sliced fermented oil bean)

Instructions

1. Wash the yam with clean water, peel the skin and cook the yam for about thirty minutes.
2. Once the yam is properly cooked, drain the remaining water and set aside.
3. In a medium saucepan, pour in the palm oil and warm over low heat. Add a pinch of salt and pepper as seasonings to taste.
4. Add an adequate amount of ukpaka and toss to combine with the oil.
5. Wash and cut the utazi leaves and add to the oil.
6. Serve the yam with the utazi sauce.

Ji agbigbu in a plantain boat

NUTRITIONAL CONTENTS:
Calories 209, total fat 3.1g 4%, sodium 35mg 1%, potassium 2,854mg 81%, total carbohydrate 129g 43%, dietary fibre 12g 124% and protein 18g 88%.

JI NMANU
(Yam & Palm Oil)

Ingredients

1. 5 cups of medium of yam, cut into cubes
2. 2 cups of spinach or garden egg leaves
3. 1 big onion
4. 2 habanero or scotch bonnet pepper
5. 2 table spoons of red palm oil
6. Salt and/or seasoning cubes

Instructions

1. Wash the habanero pepper and chop into smaller pieces.
2. Wash the vegetables and slice them into smaller pieces as well.
3. Place the palm oil in a saucepan and heat over a low fire.
4. Peel off the skin of the yam, and cut into smaller pieces. Wash the yam with clean water. Place the cubed yam in a medium-sized cooking pot, add a good quantity of water and boil over medium heat.
5. Slice the onions into chunks and add to the cooking yam.
6. Add salt to taste and cover the cooking pot. Cook the yam for twenty minutes until the yam becomes soft. Bring out the onion chunks and set aside.
7. Let the yam cool for about 5 minutes. Once the yam is cool, mash it using a potato masher or any other masher of your choice. Use a spatula to make the yam dough even smoother. Do not add more water.
8. Once the yam is completely mashed, use a deep-curved spoon to make little balls of the yam dough. Lay down spinach leaves or garden egg leaves on a kitchen table and place the yam balls on them.
9. Drizzle ground pepper and pour palm oil over the yam balls. Place the sliced vegetables on top of the balls and serve.

NUTRITIONAL CONTENTS
Calories 304.3, total fat 7.5g, saturated fat 1.5g, cholesterol 38.2mg, sodium 42.5mg potassium 1,095.1mg, total carbohydrate 53.2g, dietary fibre 6.1g, sugars 14.9g and protein 9.8g.

AKPURUAKPU JI
(Yam Balls)

Ingredients

1. 6 cups of white yam.
2. 1 table spoon finely chopped scotch bonnet pepper or ½ dry chilli pepper as desired.
3. Salt and seasoning cube as required.
4. 1½ medium red onions finely chopped or in paste form
5. Adequate oil for frying

NUTRITIONAL CONTENTS
Calories 33.58, total fat 1.48g 2%, cholesterol 54.56mg 18%, sodium 23.11mg 1%, potassium 113.4mg 2%, total carbohydrates 2.97g 1%, sugars 1.35g 5%, dietary fibre 0.63g 3% and protein 2.47g 5%.

Instructions

1. Peel the skin off the yam, cut it into smaller pieces and wash with clean water. Place the sliced yam in a medium-sized cooking pot and place the pot on the burner. Add in ingredients and the seasoning cubes and cook for about 30 minutes on medium heat. Check intermittently to avoid a possibility of the yam burning because the yam must be cooked in minimal water.
2. Place a frying pan over medium heat, and add the sliced diced onion and pepper. Fry the onions and pepper for about 7 minutes. Mash the boiled yam with salt, sautéed peppers and onions until well combined and smooth. Mould the spiced mashed yams into balls or patty shapes.
3. Place a frying pan over low heat and heat the vegetable oil. Fry the moulded balls of yam. Once the yam starts browning, stir and remove from the hot oil. Serve with any sauce of choice.

NRI ASURUASU
(Pounded Yam)

Previously there was just one way to make pounded yam, however, with the advent of technology, there are now multiple ways to do this. Below are a few ways to make pounded yam.

TYPICAL POUNDED YAM RECIPE:

Ingredients

1. Half tuber of white yam.
2. Some cups of water.

Instructions

1. Peel off the skin of the yam, and wash with clean water. Cut into sizable pieces and place in a pot. Add water and boil the yam cubes.
2. Once the yam is cooked, place in a mortar and pound until it becomes smooth. If it is hard, add some hot water to the mix and pound until well combined.
3. Serve with any soup of your choice.

ALTERNATIVE POUNDED YAM RECIPES

A) Ingredients

1. Yam flour (poundo-flour)

Instructions

1. Place the pot on heat and add water. Once the water gets to boiling point, remove some, and leave only the amount you need for the desired quantity of pounded yam.
2. Pour the poundo flour into the boiling water and stir until the paste meets the desired consistency. Continue to stir until well combined. Add a little water and allow it cook for a few minutes, then mix again until it is thoroughly evenly. Take off heat and serve with any soup of your choice.

B) Ingredients

1. Yam cut into cubes
2. Water

Instructions

1. Blend the yam cubes into a runny paste, Place pot on heat and add the paste,. continuing to stir as it cooks until it forms a thick texture. Depending on your desired texture, you can add a little water and allow it cook for a few minutes, and then mix until well combined. Take off heat and serve with any soup of your choice.

NUTRITIONAL CONTENTS
Calories 470, 9%, total fat 6g 8%, saturated fat 1.5g 0%, cholesterol 0mg 2%, sodium 50mg 34%, total carbohydrates 103g 16%, dietary fibre 4g, sugars 1g and protein 4g.

OTO
(Water Yam Dumpling)

Ingredients

1. 3 cubes of cubed water yam
2. 5 tablespoons of palm oil
3. 1 tablespoon of pepper
4. 1 tablespoon of chopped onions
5. Salt and seasoning cubes as required
6. Scent leaf and/or green pumpkin leaves

Instructions

1. Peel off the skin of the water yam, cut into smaller sizes and wash with clean water. Place the water yam cubes in batches into a blender or a food processor and blend until it becomes smooth. Alternatively, you can grate or pound the yam. When grating, chop into small sizes to allow easy grinding. Make small balls out of the water yam paste and set aside.
2. In a cooking pot, pour some cups of water and other ingredients like onions, salt, seasoning cubes and palm oil and boil over medium heat for about 3-5 minutes.
3. Once the water stock is boiled, slowly add in the water yam balls in such a way that they don't stick to one another. Cook the yam balls on low heat until the water stock thickens and the yam becomes brown in colour. Taste for seasonings and salt, add more if required. Wash and slice the scent leaves or any vegetable of choice, and add to the yam pudding. Simmer for about one minute and serve.

NUTRITIONAL CONTENTS
Calories 193, total fat 4g, cholesterol 7mg, total carbohydrate 12g, dietary fibre 2g and Protein 9g.

JI MMIRI OKU
(Yam Pepper Soup)

Ingredients

1. 1 kilogram of white puna yam
2. 1 teaspoon ground pepper
3. 15 pods of uda (grains of selim)
4. 1 teaspoon dry cayenne pepper
5. ½ tablespoon of uziza seeds (false cubeb)
6. 5 uziza leaves (false cubeb leaves)
7. ½ teaspoon ogiri Igbo
8. 5 utazi leaves.

Instructions

1. With the aid of a dry mill, properly grind ingredients like the black peppers, uda, uziza and dry cayenne pepper together.
2. Wash the uziza leaves and utazi leaves vegetables) with clean water, and slice them nto smaller pieces. Keep the vegetables aside.
3. Peel off the skin of the yam, cut into desired shapes with a knife and wash with clean water. Place the white yam into a cooking pot, and add other ingredients like the dry spices, ogiri Igbo, and salt to taste. Pour water into the pot and cook over medium heat for about thirty minutes until the yam becomes tender.
4. Once the yam is fully cooked, add the sliced vegetables and stir. Simmer for about three minutes and serve.

NUTRITIONAL CONTENTS
Calories 302.6, total tat 2.3g, cholesterol 47.6mg, sodium 73.4mg, potassium 1,415.2mg, total carbohydrate 50.9g, dietary fibre 7.4g, sugars 0.8g, protein 18.2g.

JI AHURUAHU
(Roasted Yam)

Ingredients

1. 1 small or medium size yam
2. Palm oil
3. Salt
4. Ground chili pepper
5. Onions as required

Instructions

Roasted yam can be roasted many ways. Below are a few methods.

Typical roasted yam process:

Simply make fire with wood or charcoal and place the yam on top of a grill on the fire. Depending on the size of the yam. If it is big, you can roast on each side for 30 – 40 minutes. after both sides are well roasted and the yam appears smaller in size, take off heat and let it sit for a few minutes, then peel and serve with sauce.

Oven roasted yam process:

1. Preheat oven to 450 degrees F.
2. Peel off the yam skin, cut the yam into cubes or wedges and wash with clean water.
3. Place the yam in a baking sheet together with ingredients like oil, salt, and pepper to taste.
4. Grill the yam in the oven for about 35 - 45 minutes until the yam becomes tender and browned. Remember to toss regularly.
5. Once ready, bring out from oven and serve with a simpl sauce of sautéed onions and chili peppers in palm oil.

NUTRITIONAL CONTENTS
Calories 170, total fat 1.5g, sodium 380mg 16%, carbohydrates 38g, fibre 4g 16% and protein 2g.

ACHICHA EDE
(Cocoyam Porridge)

Ingredients

1. 3 cups of achicha ede (cocoyam flakes)
2. 5 cups of any green leafy vegetables like Nigerian pumpkin leaves (ugu) or amaranth greens
3. ½ cup scent leaves
4. 1 cup of red palm oil
5. 1cup of ukpaka (sliced fermented oil bean)
6. 2 red onions
7. 4 habanero peppers to taste
8. Salt and seasoning cubes as required
9. Four cups of fio fio (pigeon pea, agbugbu)

Instructions

1. Rinse the achicha with clean water and soak in water overnight.
2. The next day, remove the achicha from the water and rinse again with clean water. Use a mortar to crush the achicha into pieces.
3. Wrap the crushed achicha in batches using uma leaves, banana leaves or any local leaves accessible to you. Place the wraps in a medium-sized cooking pot, add water to it and cook over medium heat for about 20 - 30 minutes. Once it is ready, remove the cooked achicha from the cooking pot and set aside.
4. Wash the green amaranth or pumpkin leaves or spinach and scent leaves with clean water. Cut them into smaller sizes. Slice the onions and peppers.
5. In another cooking pot, pour in the palm oil and heat over medium heat. Add the ukpaka to the hot oil and fry for about 3 minutes.
6. Add the sliced vegetables and fry for about 2 minutes, then the cooked achicha and stir appropriately. Add salt, onions and pepper. Simmer for about one minute. Serve warm.

NUTRITIONAL CONTENTS
Calories 234.58, total fat 3.48g, cholesterol 23.56mg, total carbohydrates 18.5g, dietary fibre 2g and protein 23g.

AYARAYA JI
(Pigeon Peas Porridge with Yam)

Ingredients

1. 4 cups of Nigerian fio-fio, known as pigeon peas
2. ½ small size yam
3. 1 large onion
4. A mixture of yellow pepper and red pepper or any hot pepper of choice
5. 1 tablespoonful of zziza
6. 2 cups of ukpaka (fermented sliced oil bean) or as desired
7. 1 cup of red palm oil.
8. Salt and stock cubes as desired

Instructions

1. Pick all dirt from the pigeon beans and then soak for at least 1 hour. Soaking helps get rid of the anti-nutrients and also cuts down on cooking time.
2. Place beans in a pot with adequate water, cook for about 40 minutes until the pigeon peas become tender and soft.
3. Peel the skin off the yam, cut into smaller cubes with a knife and wash with clean water. Place the cubed yam on top of the boiling pigeon peas. Cook further until the yam becomes soft. Add some salt. Simmer for two minutes and take off heat.
4. Wash and slice the onions into smaller pieces. Grind the peppers and some onions in a blender or you can use a mortar. Pound the uziza as well.
5. In another cooking pot, pour in palm oil and heat over medium heat. Once the oil is hot, add onions and pepper and fry for about two minutes. Add uziza and the stock cubes and stir again. Add the rest of the salt, then place the yam and cooked fio-fio in the oil sauce.
6. Use a spatula to stir, combining everything effectively. Simmer for about 2 minutes and serve.

Calories 312, total fat 8g, cholesterol 18mg, total carbohydrates 21g, dietary fibre 4g and protein 31g.

RICE (OSIKAPA) RECIPES

Rice as a food source, was a later discovery of the Igbo people. As a result, most of their rice recipes are cantered on the availability, accessibility and individual affordability of ingredients.

NATIVE JOLLOF RICE

Ingredients

1. 3 cups of local rice or any available rice
2. 1 tablespoon tatashe paste
3. 1 medium chopped onion and one medium onion paste
4. 1 teaspoon scotch bonnet paste or more if you wish it spicy
5. A half cup of dried hot pepper
6. ½ cup of palm oil
7. Water stock
8. 3 tablespoons of fresh locust beans known as Iru
9. One cup of spinach, pumpkin leaves or basil leaves
10. Vegetable stock cubes (optional)
11. 2 seasoning cubes
12. Salt to taste

Instructions

1. Pick out all impurities from the rice and wash the rice thoroughly. In a cooking pot, add an adequate amount of clean cooking water and boil over medium heat, while the rice is soaked in water. Once the water in the pot boils, drain water from the rice and add into the pot of hot water. Parboil for 15 minutes. Once the rice is a little soft but still hard, rinse out and drain the water. Set aside.

2. In the same cooking pot, add the palm oil and place over medium heat. Once the oil heats up, slice the onion bulb and add. Fry for about 6 - 8 minutes until the onion becomes translucent. Add the locust beans and sauté for 2 - 3 minutes until it is fragrant.

3. Add the blended peppers and onions along with the seasoning cubes and salt to taste. Stir properly and cook for about 5 -6 minutes. Add the vegetable water stock cubes and cook for another 4 minutes to integrate the ingredients. Once this is done, stir in the parboiled rice and to combine properly. Taste for salt and other seasonings, and add more if needed. Cover the cooking pot, and cook till the rice is soft and water in the pot dries up. Serve.

NUTRITIONAL CONTENTS:
Calories 443.5, total fat 14.8g, cholesterol 6.2mg, sodium 5,093.1 mg, potassium 952.6mg, total carbohydrate 69.1g, dietary fibre 3.6g, sugars 4.7g and protein 9.8g.

RICE & STEW

Ingredients

1. 4 fresh plum tomatoes
2. 3 medium onions
3. 2 cloves garlic paste (optional)
4. 1 medium ginger root
5. 6 scotch bonnets peppers
6. 5 tablespoons tomato paste
7. 1 cup of peanut oil or any oil of choice
8. Salt to taste
9. 4 teaspoons of curry powder
10. 1 tablespoon of any seasoning or stock cube

Instructions

1. Peel off the skin of the ginger, garlic, and onion, wash with clean water and slice into smaller pieces. Slice the pepper and tomato as well. Place all these ingredients in a blender or a food processor and blend very well without adding water.
2. In a large cooking pot, pour in the peanut oil and heat over medium heat. Add the blended ingredients to the hot oil and fry for about 40 minutes or until it thickens, stirring periodically to avoid burning.
3. Once the stew sauce is thick and well fried, add in the tomato paste and cook over medium heat.
4. Add other ingredients like the seasoning cubes, and salt to taste. Add in a little amount of water and let simmer for about 20 minutes. Serve with rice, yam potatoes or any other food of choice
5. Cook the white rice and get it ready.
6. Pour the prepared stew over the white rice and enjoy your meal.

NUTRITIONAL CONTENTS:
Calories 699.0, total fat 42.7g, cholesterol 146.4mg, sodium 2,553.5mg, total carbohydrates 17.4g, dietary fibre 3.4g and protein 56.4g.

COCONUT RICE

Ingredients

1. 2 tablespoons of coconut oil
2. 1 cup of diced red onions
3. 1/2 teaspoon of ground red pepper
4. 1/2 teaspoon of curry
5. 1/2 teaspoon of rosemary
6. 1/2 teaspoon of salt to taste
7. 2 seasoning cubes
8. 1 chopped scotch bonnet peppers
9. 1 cup of chopped green pepper
10. 2 cups of coconut milk
11. 1 1/2 cup of parboiled rice
12. Salt to taste

Instructions

1. Place a medium cooking pot over medium heat, add in the oil and let heat. Once the oil is hot, add in the onions and fry for a few minutes until translucent. Add in the peppers, curry, salt to taste, oregano, seasoning cubes, scotch bonnet peppers, and sweet peppers then cook for about five minutes.
2. Pour in the milk, stir properly to combine, then add in the parboiled rice. Let the rice cook for about 45 minutes then serve.

NUTRITIONAL CONTENTS:
Calories 313, fat 8.4g, carbohydrates 54g, fibre 0g, and protein 5.1g

NIGERIAN FRIED RICE

Ingredients

1. 6 cups of partially cooked rice
2. ½ cup of vegetable oil
3. 1 medium onion finely chopped
4. 2 teaspoons of minced garlic (optional)
5. 1 teaspoon of green pepper
6. ½ teaspoon of dry thyme
7. 3 teaspoon of fried rice seasoning
8. Liquid Maggi (optional)
9. 1 table teaspoon of curry powder (optional)
10. Salt to taste
11. 1 cup of peas, 1 cup of carrots, 1 cup of green beans

Instructions

1. Start by cooking the rice. Ensure it is not completely done so that a little additional heat would help it cook just right.
2. Place a medium-sized cooking pot or wok over medium heat. Add a tablespoon of vegetable oil and heat up. Place the cooked rice into the heated oil and stir vigorously for about 2-3 minutes while adding the Maggi liquid (if using) and also water to moisturize the rice. Set aside.
3. Heat a large wok or skillet over medium to high heat with 2 tablespoons of vegetable oil.
4. Once the oil is heated, add onions and sauté for about 5 minutes. Add garlic, followed by the peppers and all the other ingredients such as thyme, garlic, peas, carrots, curry powder, and seasoning cubes. Stir well for about 2 minutes until a good combination is achieved. Splash a little water to deglaze the pan.
5. Add the fried ingredients to the cooking pot containing the cooked rice and stir very well until everything is well combined. Taste for seasoning, salt and pepper and add more if needed. Serve.

NUTRITIONAL CONTENTS:
Calories 485, total fat 19g 29%, cholesterol 273mg 91%, sodium 825mg 34%, potassium 354mg 10%, carbohydrates 48g 16%, dietary fibre 3g 12% and protein 27g 54%.

BEANS (AGWA) RECIPES

Legumes are a major part of the Igbo diet. Previously plant-based eaters, beans and other forms of legumes were a major protein source in the Igbo diet.

UKWA
(African Breadfruit)

Ingredients

1. 5 cups of ukwa (African breadfruit)
2. 1 sliced green bell pepper
3. 1 sliced onion
4. 3 sliced yellow scotch bonnet peppers
5. 1/2 teaspoon of black pepper to taste
6. 3 tablespoons of palm oil.
7. 1/4 teaspoon of akanwu (potash) - this is optional.
8. 3/4 cup of sweet corn.
9. 1/2 cup of Ugba (fermented oil bean seeds)
10. 2 stock cubes.
11. Salt to taste.

Instructions

1. If using dried ukwa, soak in a bowl of cold water overnight, then wash and pick out the dirt. You don't need to soak the ukwa in water if it is fresh.
2. Place the washed ukwa into a cooking pot, pour in enough water to cover (about an inch above the ukwa level) then bring to boil. Once the breadfruit boils, add in the potash and cook for about 30 minutes or until the seeds become soft as desired without the water drying up.
3. Add in the palm oil, stock cubes, salt, and pepper to taste, stir properly to combine then cook the ukwa seeds for about 7 minutes. Add in the onion, sweet corn, Ugba, bell pepper, and scotch pepper, stir to combine then turn off the heat.
4. Let the meal sit in the covered pot for a few minutes then serve.

Bitterleaf alternative:

After the ukwa has cooked add oil, onions, ogiri, pepper, stock cubes, and salt to taste. Stir to combine, then cook for a few more minutes until the palm oil becomes yellow in colour. Add in the washed bitter leaves, and let simmer for a few minutes until the leaves wilts. Serve.

NUTRITIONAL CONTENTS:
lories 338, fat 9.g1, carbohydrates 68g.4g, fibre 12.3g, and
otein 3.8g.

BOILED BEANS

Ingredients

1. 3 cups of black-eyed beans or honey beans
2. 1 medium onion chopped
3. 1 stock cube (optional)
4. Salt to taste

Instructions

1. Place the beans in a tray and carefully pick out the stones and other unwanted particles from it.
2. Soak beans for at least 1 hour. This will help reduce the anti-nutrients, it will also rehydrate the beans as well as reduce cooking time. Place a cooking pot over high heat and pour in an adequate amount of water. Drain the soaked beans and add to the boiling water. Wait till it starts to foam. Drain off boiled water, rinse and place back in water filled pot to boil.
3. Cook beans on slow heat for about an hour or until it's becomes tender and soft.
4. Once the beans is cooked and soft you can serve with rice and stew, or just stew.

NUTRITIONAL CONTENTS:
Calories 30, sodium 5mg, carbohydrates 7g, dietary fibre 3g, sugar 3g, and protein 2g.

BEANS POTTAGE

Ingredients

1. 4 cups of honey beans or black eyed peas or as desired
2. ¼ cup palm oil
3. 3 tatashe
4. 5 scotch bonnet peppers
5. 1½ medium red onion
6. 1 clove garlic
7. 1 teaspoon uziza seeds
8. Seasoning cubes and salt to taste

Instructions

1. Place the beans in a tray and carefully pick out the stones and other unwanted particles from it.
2. Soak beans for at least 1 hour. This will help reduce the anti-nutrients, it will also rehydrate the beans as well as reduce cooking time. Place a cooking pot over high heat and pour in an adequate amount of water. Drain water and add beans to the cooking water. Wait till it starts to foam. Take off boil, drain water, rinse and place back to boil.
3. Cook beans on slow heat for about an hour.
4. While the beans is cooking use a blender, food processor or a grinding stone to blend all listed ingredients and set aside. Once the beans are completely cooked, lower the heat and pour in the blended ingredients. Cook for an additional 5 minutes then pour in the palm oil and cook for another 10 minutes until the water reduced to your desired consistency.
5. Stir properly to combine and ensure to add seasoning at the last minute of cooking, as salt may make the beans hard to cooked and difficult to digest. Add salt and other seasonings to the cooked beans as desired. Turn off the heat, and let the beans sit for 5 minutes to give a thicker texture if need be. Serve with plantain, rice or even soaked garri and enjoy.

NUTRITIONAL CONTENTS:
Calories 544.4, total fat 16.0g, cholesterol 37.7mg, sodium 7,025.1mg, potassium 1,755.3mg, total carbohydrate 78.3g, dietary fibre 19.0g, sugars 0.2g and protein 26.9g.

OKPA
(Bambara Bean Cake)

Ingredients

1. 10 cups of bambara nut flour
2. 1 ½ cups palm oil
3. 2 crushed stock cubes.
4. 1 medium grated onion.
5. 4 teaspoons ground chili pepper.
6. Salt to taste
7. Warm water as required.
8. Banana leaves or uma leaves.

Instructions

1. In a big mixing bowl, pour in the okpa flour and add in the palm oil. Wash your hands and mix the two together until the flour turns from white to yellow. You can also use a spatula for the mixing.
2. Once the flour and oil are well mixed, add in a good amount of warm water and mix again. You have to mix it well to avoid lumps. Allow the mixture sit for about an hour or 2.
3. Add in all listed ingredients and mix again.
4. Place some of the natives leaves in the pot to avoid the possibility of the okpa sticking in the pot. Add water in the pot and place on medium heat and allow boiling. Once the water is boiled, add in the wrapped okpa and cook for 1 hour 30 minutes. Intermittently check the okpa and add water necessary.
5. Once the okpa is ready, take it out from heat and let it sit for about 20 minutes. Serve.

NUTRITIONAL CONTENTS:
Calories 250, total fat 12.0g, cholesterol 18.7mg, total carbohydrate 27g, dietary fibre 7.9.0g and protein 5.4g.

MOI MOI
(Steamed Bean Pudding)

Ingredients

1. 4 cups of black-eyed beans.
2. 2 medium onions.
3. 3 big tatashe.
4. 3 scotch bonnet peppers
5. 3 tablespoons of palm oil
6. 2 seasoning and salt to taste
7. Moi moi leaves

Instructions

1. Place the beans in a tray and carefully pick out the stones and other unwanted particles from it.
2. Soak beans for at least 1 hour, it will help loosen the skin. Take off the skin completely and rinse properly.
3. Using a blender or a food processor, blend the beans and other ingredients except for palm oil and salt until the mixture becomes smooth. Add little water to make a not so thick batter.
4. In a large bowl place the beans paste and add salt, palm oil. Taste for salt and other seasonings and add more if needed.
5. Place some of the natives leaves in the pot to avoid the possibility of the moi moi sticking in the pot. Add water in the pot, place on medium heat and allow to boil. Once the water is boiled, add in the wrapped moi moi and cook for 1 hour 30 minutes. Intermittently check the moi moi and add water necessary.
6. Once the moi moi is ready, take it out from heat and let it sit for about 20 minutes. Serve.

NUTRITIONAL CONTENTS:
Calories 119.2, total fat 4.7g, cholesterol 58.9mg, sodium 263.2mg, potassium 325.3mg, total carbohydrate 13.9g, dietary fibre 4.4g and protein 6.9g.

CASSAVA RECIPES

AKPU
(Cassava Fufu)

Ingredients

1. Cassava
2. Water
3. Sieve
4. Muslin bag

Instructions

1. Peel the skin of the cassava and wash it with with clean water. Place the peeled cassava in a large basin and cover it with water. Soak it for 5 of days for fermentation to take place. Make sure you change the water every day.
2. On the sixth day, remove the cassava from water and cut into smaller pieces. By this time, the cassava is already very soft. Place the cassava in batches into a colander, place in a bowl and add water to it as you wash the cassava into the bowl, leaving the chaff in the colander. Pour the cassava liquid into a muslin bag and let water drain. To drain the water effectively place heavy objects on the muslin bag. Once the cassava is properly drained and become solid you can now place in a bowl and use hand to knead it and then place it in a motar and pound until very smooth. Place a pot over medium heat; line the bottom of the pot with a muslin bag or some leaves (the same used in wrapping okpa or moi moi. Make the cassava into small to medium (depending on the quantity and size of pot) oval shapes and place in the pot. Cover pot and allow to cook for 40 minutes over medium heat. Take out and pound, then repeat the cooking process again. Finally take off heat pour into the mortar and pound for the last time and its ready to eat. Another method would be to place pot on heat with water, once the water is boiled, add in the desired amount of cassava fufu. Add a little amount of hot water to the fufu and carry out a continuous stir for about 10 - 15 minutes using a spatula. Keep stirring until the fufu looks cooked
3. Once the fufu is ready, make into medium oval shapes and wrap with thin cellophane bags and serve with any soup of choice.

NUTRITIONAL CONTENTS:
Calories 267, protein 2g, total fat 1.2g, and carbohydrates 84g.

ABACHA
(African Salad)

Ingredients

1. 2 cups of abacha (Igbo dried shredded cassava)
2. ¼ cup palm oil
3. ¼ teaspoon akaun (cooking potash.)
4. 2 scotch bonnet peppers finely chopped
5. I small onions sliced in rings
6. ¼ cup garden egg leaves sliced.
7. 2 wraps of ogiri
8. 1 seasoning cube and salt to taste.

Instructions

1. Wash the garden egg leaf with clean water and cut into smaller pieces and set aside.
2. Boil water. Rinse the abacha with hot water and salt and place in a colander for the water to drain.
3. Place a medium cooking pot on low heat and set aside to cool.
4. Place the akaun on a small deep plate and dissolve with little hot water. Combine the dissolved akaun with the heated palm oil and mix well. Add in other ogiri, pepper seasoning cube and salt to taste. Finally add in the abacha and mix thoroughly. Serve with onion rings and sliced garden egg leaves.

NUTRITIONAL CONTENTS:
Calories 358.3, protein 14.3g, total fat 0.5g, dietary fibre 0.7g, and carbohydrates 22.7g.

GARRI
(Cassava Flakes)

Ingredients

1. Cassava
2. Water.

Instructions

1. Peel off the skin of the cassava tubers with the aid of a kitchen knife and wash them with clean water. Cut the cassava into smaller sizes and blend them in a grinding machine. After the grinding process, the cassava is usually placed in a jack to completly dry them. This might take about two to three days.
2. Once the cassava is dried, use a sieve to separate the cassava powder from other particles.
3. Place a wide cassava frying pan on high heat and fry the cassava for about 30 minutes until the cassava becomes very dry, brittle and flaky.
4. Once the garri is processed, store in a bag and keep away from moisture. You can either drink it with water and sugar or make it into eba which is served with various soup.

NUTRITIONAL CONTENTS:
Calories 436 1%, total fat 0.4g 1%, saturated fat 0.1g 0%, cholesterol 0mg 3%, sodium 67mg, dietary fibre 7.2g , Sugars 4.3g and Protein 8.4g.

BOILED CASSAVA

Ingredients

1. 1 large cassava tubers.
2. Salt to taste
3. Pepper to taste
4. Palm oil(optional)

Instructions

1. Peel the skin of the cassava tubers and wash with clean water and then divide into four equal sections.
2. In a cooking pot, pour in an adequate amount of water and bring to boil over medium heat. Once the water is hot, add in the cut cassava tubers and boil for 30 minutes or until it become tender and soft. Once the cassava is cooked, remove from heat and drain the water.
3. Serve in a clean plate with some sprinkles of salt and chili pepper. You can use some palm oil if desired.

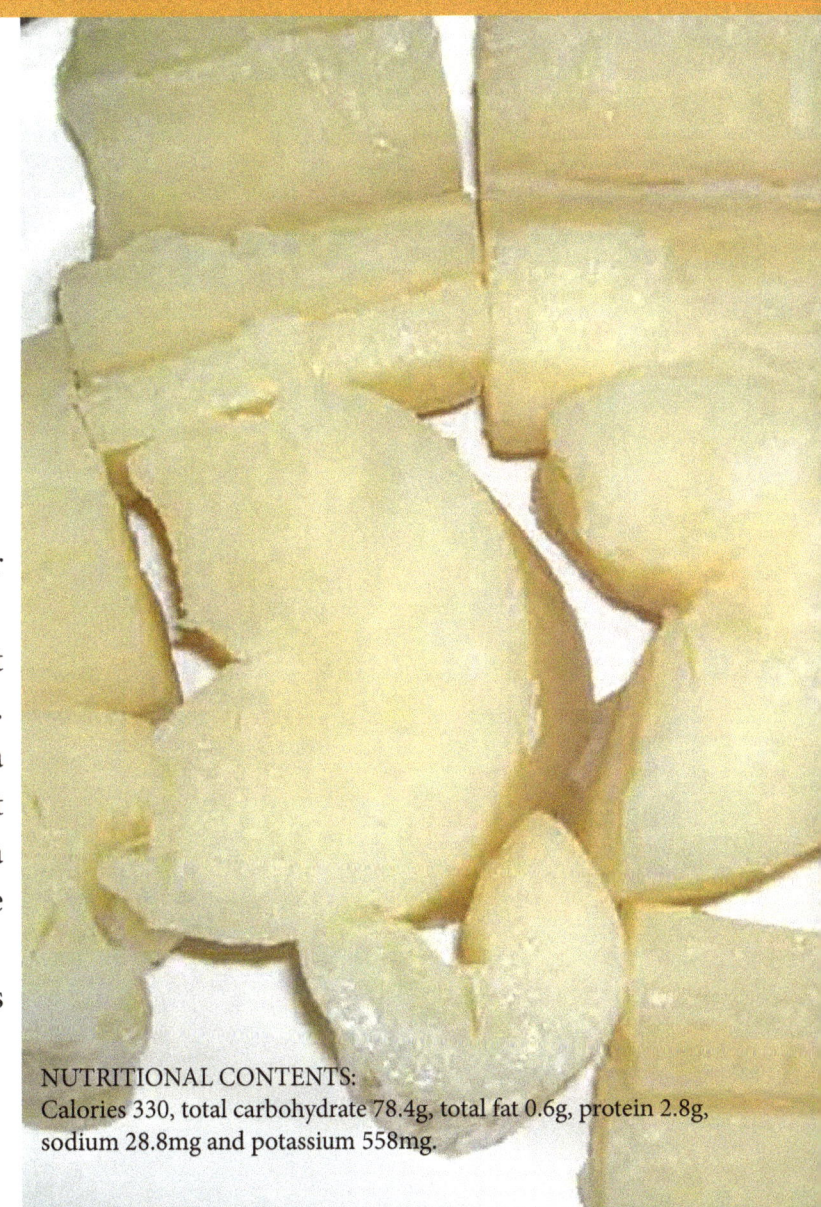

NUTRITIONAL CONTENTS:
Calories 330, total carbohydrate 78.4g, total fat 0.6g, protein 2.8g, sodium 28.8mg and potassium 558mg.

MAIZE/CORN RECIPES

NRI OKA
(Corn Moi Moi)

Ingredients

1. 4 medium capsicum finely chopped (tatashe)
2. 4 red scotch bonnet peppers
3. 1 medium onion chopped.
4. 10 pieces of small fresh corn on the cob
5. 2 stock cubes.
6. 1 teaspoon of salt or as required.
7. ½ cup palm oil
8. Native leaves

Instructions

1. Wash the red bell peppers, bonnet peppers and onion in clean water and place them in a blender or a food processor with a little water or pound in a motar. Blend until the ingredients become smooth, pour into a small bowl and set aside.
2. Remove the kernels of corn from its cob with the aid of a knife and place in a blender or a food processor in batches or in two equal halves with a little addition of water. Blend until the corn becomes smooth. Place the blended corn kernels with the blended ingredients and mix properly. When this is done, add the stock cubes, salt to taste and palm oil and mix again to properly combine. Taste seasonings and add more if needed.
3. Wrap up the mixture in the native leaves. Place a big cooking pot over medium heat and add a small amount of water. Once the water is hot, place the wrapped corn mixture into the pot, cover and cook for about 40 minutes adding more water once the previous one becomes dry.
4. Once the corn mixture is ready, take it out of the heat and let sit for about twenty minutes then serve.

NUTRITIONAL CONTENTS:
Calories 421, total fat 14g 22%, saturated fat 5g 25%, sodium 827mg 34and potassium 743mg 21%. total carbohydrates 67g 22%, dietary fibre 8g 32%, sugars 10g and protein 10g 20%.

OKA NA UBE
(Boiled Corn & Pear)

Ingredients

1. 2 sweet corns.
2. 3 African pears known as ube.
3. Salt as to taste.

Instructions

1. In a big cooking pot, add in water and allow to boil for about 10 minutes over medium heat. Once the water is boiled, add in a pinch of salt and the sweet corns and cook the corn for about 50 minutes (depending on the size of the corn and texture, it may take longer) or until it becomes tender. Once the corn is cooked, drain out the water and place the cooked corn in a bowl.
2. Using the same salty hot water from the corn, place in the African pears and soak of a few minutes until it becomes tender.
3. Once the pears are softened, take them out of the hot water and serve with the soft sweet corns.

NUTRITIONAL CONTENTS:
Calories 860, total fat 82.8g 262%, saturated fat 52.4g 72%, Cholesterol 215mg 27%, sodium 658mg 37%, total carbohydrates 110.9g 23%, dietary fibre 5.8g, sugars 14.1g and protein 4.8g.

AKAMU
(African Custard)

Akamu, known as African custard can be made with different grains. For this particular recipe we will use corn. To make akamu (corn custard) from scratch is very easy. All you need is dry corn, fine chiffon cloth, muslin bag, a blender and water.

Instructions

Instructions: Pick out the dirt from the corn and wash properly. And then soak the corn in a generous amount of cold water for three to four days. You must replace the water with fresh water every day. On the third or fourth day blend the corn into a fine paste. Drape the chiffon cloth over a big bowl and tie it up. Sieve the corn paste by pouring water on it until you are left with the chaff. This can be done in batches. When done, set the liquid aside to settle for at least 3 hours. Drain the clear water, and then pour the remaining paste/liquid into a muslin bag. Tie the muslin cloth and place some weight to strain the last bit of water, and then leave overnight to ferment. By morning, your corn custard should be ready.

Ingredients (for the final corn custard)

1. 1 ½ cup akamu(pap)
2. 3 cups of boiling water.
3. Sweetener of choice.

Instructions

1. Start by boiling 3 cups of water in a kettle over medium heat.
2. In a small bowl, place the pap paste (akamu) and add a little amount of water at room temperature. Stir both of them until the mixture becomes completely smooth in a medium runny consistency.
3. Once water is fully boiled, add to the akamu mix while stirring with a spoon. Stop once the pap becomes thick. Add in any sweetener of your choice and serve with moimoi, akara or bread.

NUTRITIONAL CONTENTS
Calories 200, total carbohydrates 46.7g 17%.

125

AGIDI
(Savoury Corn Starch Jello)

Ingredients

1. 1 cup of corn flour or corn starch.
2. Water as required.
3. Agidi wrapping leaves (same like okpa leave).

Instructions

1. In a large mixing bowl, pour in the corn flour and add a desirable amount of water, little by little until a good consistency is achieved without lumps. Don't add all the water at once.
2. Pour in the corn mixture in a cooking pot and place over medium heat setting. Stir the corn paste consistently with a wooden spoon or a spatula until a thick corn mixture is achieved. Do not stop stirring to avoid lumps.
3. Once the corn mixture becomes as thick as custard, add in some water and allow it to simmer over medium heat for about 10 minutes. Mix the agidi and water properly by stirring. Once the elapse of 10 minutes, check if the agidi is properly cooked by placing a small portion of it in cold water. If it sets, it is ready.
4. Place the agidi in batches into the native leaves, wrap and set aside to cool for about 10 minutes at room temperature. Once set, serve with stew or any preferred side.

NUTRITIONAL CONTENTS:
Calories 211, sodium 14mg, total fat 2g, protein 4g, total carbohydrates 45g and dietary fibre 4g.

ABRIKA (PLANTAIN) RECIPES

ABRIKA AGWORO AGWO
(Plantain Pottage)

Ingredients

1. 2 unripe plantains
2. 1 cup of shredded spinach
3. 1 1/2 spoons of blended red bell pepper (optional)
4. 1 yellow pepper (optional)
5. 1 red scotch bonnet pepper
6. 2 chopped onions
7. Seasoning cubes of your choice
8. 2 cups of water.
9. 1/2 teaspoon of chili powder
10. Sea salt to taste
11. 1 cooking spoon of palm oil.

Instructions

1. Wash the plantain properly and peel off the skin using a knife. Cut the plantain into small pieces and place them into a cooking pot.
2.. Add the onion, pepper, seasoning cubes, salt, blended bell pepper and then bring to boil for about 5 minutes until it becomes soft.
3. Once the plantain is cooked and soft, add the spinach and simmer for 5 minutes over lower heat.

NUTRITIONAL CONTENTS:
Calories 280, fat 7.4g, cholesterol 30.6g, sodium 40g, carbohydrates 13g, protein 6g.

UKPO OGEDE
(Plantain Moi Moi)

Ingredients

1. 2 overripe plantains
2. 1/2 cup of palm oil
3. 1 chopped onion
4. Pepper to taste
5. Salt to taste
6. 1 vegetable stock cube
7. Water

Instructions

1. Wash and peel the skin off the plantains. Using a kitchen knife, cut the plantain into smaller sizes. Add the plantain into a blender along with onion, pepper, and vegetable cube then blend till smooth.
2. Pour the mixture into a medium mixing bowl. Add in salt to taste and palm oil, then mix thoroughly. Feel free to add a little warm water to thin out the paste if it is too thick.
3. Pour the mixture into moi moi muffin cups then set aside. Place a cooking pot over medium heat, add in about four cups of water then bring to boil. Place the muffin cups into the bot and cook the moi moi for about 25 minutes. Make sure to add more water along the way when it dried up.
4. Once it is cooked, remove from the heat and allow to cool down completely for about 5 minutes before serving.

NUTRITIONAL CONTENTS:
Calories 240, carbohydrates 48g, fat 4g, and protein 3g.

OGEDE
(Roasted Plantain)

Ingredients

1. 2 medium size plantains
2. Palm oil
3. Salt
4. Ground chili pepper
5. Onions as required

Instructions

Roasted plantain can be roasted many ways. Below are a few methods.

Typical roasted plantain process:

Simply make fire with wood or charcoal. Peel skin off plantains and place on top of a grill on the fire and roast on each side for 30 minutes. After both sides are well roasted, take off heat and let sit for a few minutes, then serve with sauce.

Oven roasted plantain process:

1. Preheat oven to 450 degrees F.
2. Peel off the plantain skin, cut long wedges and wash with clean water.
3. Place the plantains in a baking sheet together with ingredients like oil, salt, and pepper to taste.
4. Grill the plantains in the oven for about 35 minutes until the plantains become tender and browned. Remember to toss regularly.
5. Once ready, bring out from oven and serve with a simpl sauce of sautéed onions and chili peppers in palm oil.

ABRIKA EGHERE EGHE
(Fried Plantain Chips)

Ingredients

1. 2 large plantains.
2. Olive oil for deep frying.
3. Salt to taste.
4. Black pepper to taste

Instructions

1. Use a knife to peel off the skin of the plantain then slice them into small/thin and long stripes. Place the thin-sliced plantain into a large bowl, add some sprinkles of salt and pepper to taste then toss to combine. Place a skillet pan over medium heat then add in enough oil (for deep frying) then let heat.
2. Add in the sliced plantains into the hot oil and fry for a few minutes until they become golden and crispy. Once fried, place the plantains on a paper towel-lined plate then serve.

NUTRITIONAL CONTENTS:
Calories: 87, carbohydrates: 22g, protein: 0g, Fat: 0g, and fibre: 1

OTHER IGBO DISHES

NKWOBI
(African Salad)

Ingredients

1. 2 cups of mixed mushrooms
2. 1 cup of cooked seitan (optional)
3. 1 tablespoon of grapeseed oil
4. 1/4 cup of palm oil
5. 1 tablespoon of powdered potash (akanwu)
6. 1 teaspoon of ground ehuru seeds (calabash nutmeg)
7. 2 chopped scotch bonnet peppers (garnish)
8. 2 sliced onions (split into equal halves. 1 for garnish, 1 for saute)
9. 1/2 cup of ugba
10. 1 stock cube
11. Salt to taste

Instructions

1. Place a dry pan over medium heat, add grapeseed oil and let it heat up for 1 minute. Once the oil is hot, add half of the onion and sauté for a few minutes. Add the mushrooms, a pinch of salt and ¼ teaspoon ground pepper to taste. Stir-fry for 5 minutes or until cooked thoroughly. Then set aside.
2. Using a medium mixing bowl, add the powdered powdered potash and a ¼ cup of water. Mix properly to combine and sieve chaff from the mixture with a fine sieve then set aside.
3. Pour the palm oil into a dry cooking pot, add the sieved potash liquid and stir until the mixture becomes yellow and creamy. Add ugba, stock cube, ehuru and a pinch of salt then stir properly till well mixed. Add the cooked mushrooms and cooked seitan.
4. Take the nkwobi off the heat and garnish with onions, scotch bonnet and utazi leaves.
5. Enjoy.

NUTRITIONAL CONTENTS:
Calories 122, Protein 2.5g, Carbohydrate 13.2g, and fat 6.2g.

AKPURAKPU EGUSI
(Savoury Egusi Cake)

Ingredients

1. 1 tablespoons of usu for thickening (or as required depending on the quantity of the egusi)
2. 1 cup of ground egusi
3. Dry or fresh pepper to taste
4. Salt

Instructions

1. Place the above-listed ingredients in a bowl and whizz together until the egusi forms a dough. Once the blades of the chopper bowl can no longer spin the dough, transfer to a mortar and finish it.
2. With clean hands, make smaller balls out of the egusi dough and squeeze tightly to extract excess oil that may be found in it until the balls start to feel dry.
3. Once the oil has been extracted, flatten the egusi balls one after the other and place on a baking sheet and bake or pan back in an iron skillet. Once cooked it can be eaten on its own as a snack or introduced to different dishes as a meat substitute in soups like ofe okazi and even in egusi soup.

NUTRITIONAL CONTENTS
Calories 216, 28g protein, 2.7g fibre, and 21g carbohydrate

OKWA/OSE OJI
(Spicy Peanut Butter)

Ingredients

1. 3 ½ cups of toasted groundnut or salted peanut butter.
2. 1 teaspoons of ground calabash nutmeg.
3. 1 tablespoon of dry ground cayenne pepper.
4. 1 teaspoon uziza seed (optional)
5. 1 taespoon ginger powder (optional)

Instructions

1. In a grinder, add in all the ingredients and grind or pound in a mortar until all ingredients are well incorporated. Taste for salt and add more if necessary.
2. If using peanut butter - in a medium bowl add in all the dry ingredients and mix properly. Whip the peanut butter in a stand mixer for about two minutes. Once it is properly mixed, add in the dry ingredients and mix into the peanut butter. Mix all of them together until they are fully incorporated.
3. You can add more oil to the peanut butter if it becomes too dry.
4. Serve with garden egg.

NUTRITIONAL CONTENTS:
Calories 188, total fat 16g 24%, cholesterol 0mg 0%, sodium 5mg 0%, potassium 208mg 5%, total carbohydrate 6g 2%, dietary fibre 1.9g 7%, sugar 3g and protein 8g 16%.

IHE NDORI
(Vegetable Sauce)

Ingredients

1. 2 cooking spoons of vegetable oil.
2. 5 spring of onions.
3. 8 fresh and de-seeded plum tomatoes.
4. 8 medium carrots.
5. 1 small cabbage.
6. 3 medium Irish potatoes.
7. 1 red bell pepper (optional.)
8. 1 green bell pepper.
9. Salt to taste (or as required).
10. 3 seasoning cubes.

Instructions

1. Wash the plum tomatoes, carrots, cabbage and bell pepper in clean water and cut them into smaller pieces. Place the sliced ingredients in a bowl and set aside.
2. Peel the Irish potatoes, wash with clean water and cut into smaller pieces. Use a blender or a food processor to blend the potatoes into a thick paste then set aside.
3. Place a cooking pot over medium heat; add in water, chopped spring onions, seasoning cubes, and thyme. Cover the cooking pot and boil the mixture for about 10 minutes. Once the water boils, add in salt to taste, chopped tomatoes and the vegetable oil. Cook for 15 more minutes, add in the carrots and cook for an additional 5 minutes.
4. An extra five minutes later, add the rest of the ingredients like potato puree, chopped bell peppers, and cabbage. Stir properly, cover and allow to cook for about five minutes on high heat. Add more salt if needed and serve with rice.

NUTRITIONAL CONTENTS
Calories 58.8, total carbohydrate 14.1g, total fat 0.4g, protein 3.2g, potassium 811mg and Sodium 1284mg.

CONTEMPORARY DISHES

The following recipes were originally non-Igbo dishes that igbo people have come to love and enjoy.

JOLLOF SPAGHETTI

Ingredients

1. 2 cups of roasted peanuts.
2. 4 tablespoons of smoked paprika.
3. 3 tablespoons of ground ginger.
4. 2 tablespoons of ground cayenne pepper.
5. 2 tablespoons of garlic powder.
6. 3 tablespoons of onion powder.
7. 1 tablespoon of vegetable bouillon.

Instructions

1. Using a food processor or a high-speed blender, add in the tomatoes, onions, and peppers then blend until the mixture becomes smooth. Place a cooking pot over medium-high heat, add in the blended mixture then boil for about 10 - 20 minutes to reduce the paste in half. Make sure you stir the sauce as you cook.
2. Next, add in the stock, oil, thyme, curry powder, and bouillon then stir properly to combine. Next, decrease the heat to medium-low, break in the spaghetti then cook for about five minutes. Use a spatula to stir the pasts then cook for an additional 8 - 10 minutes until cooked through.
3. Add in the basil, stir to combine then serve.

NUTRITIONAL CONTENTS:
Calories: 381, carbohydrates: 78g, protein: 13g, fat: 2g, and fibre 6g.

KOKORO
(Cornmeal Snack)

Kokoro is a snack made from cornmeal.

Ingredients

1. 2 cups of dried cornmeal.
2. 1 teaspoon of cayenne pepper.
3. 1 teaspoon of ginger powder.
4. 1/3 cup of sugar or sweetener of choice.

Instructions

1. Properly sieve the cornmeal to remove all grits then pour it into a mixing bowl. Add in the sugar (or sweetener), ginger powder, and cayenne pepper then mix properly to combine. Set aside. Place a cooking pot over medium-low heat, add in 2 cups of water alongside 1/3 of the cornmeal mixture then stir to combine until it becomes a firm dough.
2. Place the dough onto a kitchen worktop surface, then let cool for a few minutes. Pour the rest of the cornmeal mixture over the dough then knead with your hands. Dust your hands with cornmeal then roll the dough into small and long sticks.
3. Place a skillet pan over medium heat, pour in enough vegetable oil for frying then let it heat. Add in the rolled-up dough and fry for a few minutes until they become brown in color. Serve.

YAAJI
(Suya Spice)

Yaaji a.k.a suya spice is a popular meat rub, can also elevate the taste of any roasted vegetable. Add to roasted mushroom for a delicious snack.

Ingredients

1. 2 cups of roasted peanuts.
2. 4 tablespoons of smoked paprika
3. 3 tablespoons of ground ginger
4. 2 tablespoons of ground cayenne pepper
5. 2 tablespoons of garlic powder
6. 3 tablespoons of onion powder
7. 1 tablespoon of vegetable bouillon

Instructions

1. Using a food processor, add in the roasted peanuts then blend (do not blend into a paste). Pour the blended peanut into a kitchen towel then squeeze out any present oil. Use your fingers to loosen up the dried peanut then pour into a mixing bowl.

2. Add in the rest of the yaaji ingredients then mix properly to combine. To have a smoother spice blend, sieve the yaaji, then use as desired.

NUTRITIONAL CONTENTS:
100g serving: calories 37, carbohydrates: 7.41g, protein: 100g serving: calories 37, carbohydrates: 7.41g, protein: 0.43g, fat: 0.65g, fiber: 0.3 0.43g, fat: 0.65g, f fibre: 0.3 g.

KULI KULI
(Peanut Cake)

Ingredients

1. 4 cups of roasted peanuts
2. A pinch of dried chili to taste
3. A pinch of dried ginger (optional)
4. 1/4 cup of water
5. Salt to taste
8. ¼ teaspoon of curry powder
9. 3 cups of water

Instructions

1. Place the roasted peanuts, chili, and ginger into a grinder and blend (do not add water). Pour the peanut paste into a mixing bowl, and then add water. Mix with a stand mixer for about one minute until smooth. Add in salt to taste then knead the batter until the oil is fully extracted.
2. Pour the extracted oil into a skillet pan then heat (do not add additional oil). Use clean hands to mold the peanut mixture into cookie shapes. Place the peanut cookies into the oil and fry for a few minutes until they become crunchy and brown in colour.
3. Serve.

NUTRITIONAL CONTENTS:
Calories: 138, carbohydrates: 21g, protein: 3g, fat: 5g, and fibre: 1g.

PUFF-PUFF

Ingredients

1. 2 cups of warm water.
2. 2 teaspoons of active dry yeast.
3. 3 cups of all-purpose flour.
4. ½ cup of sugar or sweetener of choice.
5. ½ tablespoons of salt to taste.
6. Oil for deep frying.

Instructions

1. Using a medium mixing bowl, add in the salt, sugar, water, and yeast then mix properly to combine. Let the mixture sit for about 5 minutes. Next, add in the flour then mix again to combine. Let the mixture sit for another 1 - 2 hours to rise.
2. Place a saucepan over medium heat, add in about 3-inches of vegetable oil then let it heat up until hot. Use a small kitchen spoon to scoop the batter into the hot oil in such a way that they form small balls. Fry the puff-puff for a few minutes until they become golden-brown in color.
3. Flip the puff-puff over and fry for a few more minutes until all sides turn golden brown. Once cooked, take the balls out of the oil then place them on a paper towel-lined plate. Serve.

NUTRITIONAL CONTENTS:
Calories: 138, carbohydrates: 21g, protein: 3g, fat: 5g, and fibre: 1g.

SHUKU SHUKU
(Coconut Cookies)

Ingredients

1. 1/2 pounds of grated coconut or dried shredded coconut.
2. 1/2 pound of cassava root.
3. 1/2 cup of caster sugar or sweetener of choice.

Instructions

1. Use a knife to peel off the skin of the cassava root then grate. Place the cassava in a cheesecloth, then squeeze out any present water/moisture and starch, set aside in a bowl. Use a food processor or blender to grate the coconut. Pour the coconut into the bowl containing the grated cassava roots, add in the sugar then mix everything properly to combine.
2. Preheat the oven to 350 degrees F, pour the mixture into muffin tins then bake in the oven for about 20 minutes. Flip the cookies over and cook for an additional 10 minutes until baked through.
3. Once baked, take the cookies out of the oven, add some sprinkles of confectioner's sugar then serve.

NUTRITIONAL CONTENTS:
Calories: 123, carbohydrates: 13g, protein: 2g, fat: 7g, and fibre: 1g.

VEGAN MEAT PIE

Ingredients

For the pastry:
1. 4 cups of plain flour
2. 1 teaspoon of salt to taste
3. 1 teaspoon of baking powder
4. ½ teaspoon of curry powder
5. 1 cup unmelted plant margarine
6. ¼ cup of melted plant margarine for brushing
7. ¼ cup of cold water

For the filling:
1. 2 tablespoons of plant margarine
2. 1 large and sliced onion
3. ½ pound of vegan minced meat(soya) / mushroom
4. 1 diced potato
5. 1 diced carrot
6. Salt and pepper to taste
7. 1 teaspoon of dried thyme
8. 2 tablespoons of cornflour
9. 1 cup of vegetable stock

Instructions

1. Preheat the oven to 350 degrees F. Using a large mixing bowl, add in the flour, salt to taste, baking powder, and curry powder then mix properly to combine. Add in the cubed vegan margarine then use your hands to work it in until the mixture becomes crumbly. Add in the cold water then mix to combine until a dough form.
2. Wrap the dough with a plastic wrap and refrigerate for about 30 minutes. In the meantime, make the pie filling. Place a skillet pan over medium heat, add in 2 tablespoons of the margarine then heat. Add in the onions and cook for about 4 - 5 minutes until it becomes translucent.
3. Add in the minced vegan meat, diced potato, carrot, thyme, salt, and pepper to taste, stir to combine then cook for about 5 minutes. Make sure you stir as you cook. In the meantime, pour the stock into a bowl, add in the cornflour then mix properly to combine. Pour the mixture into the pan then simmer

for about 10 -15 minutes until the sauce thickens, set aside.

4. Use a knife to divide the dough into ten balls. Working with a dough ball at a time, roll out with a rolling pin then pat the edges with little water. Pour about two tablespoons of the prepared filling at the middle of the dough then fold. Use a fork to crimp the edges of the dough together, then poke small holes at the top.

5. Line a baking tray with foil then place the filled dough on it. Brush each dough with melted margarine then bake the meat pies in the preheated oven for about 25 - 30 minutes. Serve.

NUTRITIONAL CONTENTS:
Calories 278.6, fat 16.7g, carbohydrate 28.9g, fiber 2.4g, and protein 4.4g.

CHIN CHIN

Ingredients

1. 10.58 oz. of wholemeal flour.
2. 2 tablespoons of potato starch.
3. 3.53 oz. of erythritol or stevia.
4. 1 teaspoon of baking powder.
5. 1/4 teaspoon of salt to taste.
6. 1 teaspoon of nutmeg.
7. 1 lemon.
8. 1.76 fl. oz. of canola oil.
9. 5.28 fl. oz. of almond milk.

Instructions

1. Using a large mixing bowl, add in the flour, starch, erythritol, baking powder, salt to taste, and nutmeg then mix properly to combine. Add in the lemon zest, oil, and milk then mix again to combine until a sticky dough form. Feel free to add in more milk if the dough turns out too dry, and more flour if the dough is too wet.
2. Knead the dough for a few more minutes then use clean hands to roll the dough into a ball. Place the dough ball into a bowl and refrigerate for about 5 - 10 minutes. Place the dough between two sheets of parchment paper then roll out. Use a wheel cutter to cut the dough into small squares, set aside.
3. Line a baking tray with baking paper or parchment paper, place the chin chin dough onto the tray then brush with little oil. Preheat the oven to 375 degrees F, place the baking tray into the oven and bake the chin chin for about 20 minutes until they become golden and crispy.
4. Once baked, place the baked chin chin on a wire rack to cool for a few minutes then serve.

NUTRITIONAL CONTENTS:
Calories 150, carbohydrates 20.2g, fats 5.5g, proteins 5.1g, and fibre 3.6g.

VEGAN MUSHROOM SUYA

Ingredients

1. 2 cups of oyster mushrooms.
2. ½ teaspoon of dried red chilies.
3. ½ teaspoon of ground ginger.
4. 2 teaspoons of ground roasted peanuts (optional).
5. ½ teaspoon of garlic.
6. 1 teaspoon of paprika.
7. ¼ teaspoon of salt to taste.
8. ½ teaspoon of onion.
9. 1 bouillon cube.

Instructions

1. Preheat the oven to 350 degrees F, wash the mushrooms with clean water then dry them with paper towels. Place the mushrooms in a baking pan then place the pan into the preheated oven. Bake the mushrooms for about 10 minutes then set aside.
2. Using a small mixing bowl, add in the chilies, paprika, garlic, ginger, onion, salt to taste, and bouillon cube in a dry bowl then mix properly to combine. Sprinkle the mixed spices over the cooked mushrooms then serve.

'INDOMIE' PEPPER SOUP

Ingredients

1. 2 packets (50g) of noodles.
2. 1 teaspoon of pepper soup spice.
3. Blended pepper to taste.
4. 1 sliced onion.
5. 2 minced cloves of garlic.
6. 1 handful of sliced scent leaves.
7. 1 handful uziza leaves
8. ¼ teaspoon of curry powder.
9. 3 cups of water.

Instructions

1. Place a cooking pot over medium heat, add in the water and bring to boil. Add in the indomie spices, pepper, curry, pepper soup spice, garlic, and onions, stir properly to combine then cook for about 2 minutes.
   Add in the noodles then cook for an additional 2 minutes.
2. Add in the scent leaf and cook for another 30 seconds. Serve.

NUTRITIONAL CONTENTS:
calories: 138, carbohydrates: 21g, protein: 3g, fat: 5g, and fibre 1g.

MEDICINAL JUICES & TEAS

ONUGBO JUICE
(Bitter Leaf Drink)

Bitter leaves have been used for centuries as a treatment for malaria, typhoid, diabetes, diarrhoea, and tuberculosis. Contains vitamins A, C, E, B1, B2.

Ingredients

1. A handful of fresh bitter leaves
2. 1 cup of water.

Instructions

1. Using a large mixing bowl, add in water and the bitter leaves. Then wash to remove any present dirt (make sure you select and discard diseased or yellow leaves). Using a food processor or a high-speed blender, add in the cup of water and the washed leaves, then blend until the mixture becomes a fine texture.
2. Strain the bitter leave juice using a cheesecloth, then serve in cups.

UGU & PINEAPPLE JUICE
(Pumpkin Leaf & Pineapple)

Rich in vitamins A, B1, B2, B3, B6, C, and known to aid in the maintenance of the digestive system.

Ingredients

1. Ugu (pumpkin) leaves
2. 1 small pineapple.
3. 2 limes.
4. 1/2 cup of water

Instructions

1. Using a large mixing bowl, add in water and the ugu leaves then wash to remove any present dirt and sand. Use a sharp knife to cut the pineapple into smaller chunks then place into a food processor. Add in the ugu leaves and squeeze in lime juice, then blend until the mixture becomes smooth.
2. Let the juice chill in the fridge for a few minutes then serve.

AJU MBAISE
(Brewed Traditional Leaves)

High in antioxidants, aju mbaise can aid in slowing down the ageing process. It detoxes and promotes weight loss.

Ingredients

1. 5-6 ginger roots.
2. A bunch of Mbaise traditional leaves (guava leaves, utazi leaves, ginger lily, bitter leave, paw paw leaves, scent leaves, and moringa leaves)
3. 1 tablespoon of uziza seeds.
4. 5 pods of uda seeds.
5. The back of mbaise medicinal tree (mbaise tree).

Instructions

1. Place the leaves on a flat platform, top with the rest of the ingredients then wrap together, forming a coil. Use a thigh rope to hold the medicinal herb together then use a desired.

NCHANWU JUICE
(Scent Leaf Drink)

Used in the treatment of colds and fever, as well as in relieving bloating, diarrhoea and vomiting.

Ingredients

1. 1-2 bunches of (nchanwu) scent leaves.
2. Salt to taste which is optional.

Instructions

1. Using a large mixing bowl, add in water and salt, then wash the leaves, removing all dirt and sand, then set aside. Using a food processor or a high-speed blender, add in the leaves and little water then blend until the mixture becomes smooth. Sieve the juice with cheesecloth then serve in a glass cup.

AKI ILU JUICE
(Bitter Kola Drink)

Considered as an aphrodisiac, bitter kola has been used over the years to fight infections, from the common cold, to hepatitis.

Ingredients

1. 1 crushed bitter kola.
2. 6 crushed uda seeds.
3. 40g of ginger.
4. 500ml of water.

Instructions

1. Using a motor and pistol, add in the bitter kola, uda seeds, and ginger then crush. Place the crushed ingredients into a saucepan and place over medium-low heat. Add in water then bring to boil for about 6 minutes. Once the mixture boils, pour the juice (the entire content of the saucepan) into a food processor and blend until you get a coarse texture.

2. Strain the liquid with a cheesecloth or a strainer then pour the liquid back into the saucepan. Simmer the juice for a few minutes then serve.

TIGER NUT JUICE

Rich in fibre, tiger nut can prevent constipation and aid digestion.

Ingredients

1. 1 cup of tiger nuts (soaked overnight if dry).
2. 4 cups of water or milk.
3. 6 dates as a sweetener.
4. 1/2 of a coconut.

Instructions

1. Using a food processor or a high-speed blender, add in the soaked nuts, water, coconut and dates. Blend until the mixture becomes smooth. Strain the liquid with a cheesecloth or a strainer then pour the liquid into a bowl.
2. Let the juice chill in the fridge for a few minutes, shake, and drink.

NGWO
(Palm Wine)

Palm wine contains riboflavin, which is also known as vitamin B2. Riboflavin is an antioxidant which can protect against free radicals. Can also help in maintaining a good eye sight.

Instructions

1. The palm wine tapping process: when on the tree, use a sharp knife to cut out some of the palm tree branches in other to expose the tissue then cut 10-12 cm deep into the tree. Place a hollow bamboo stick at the point of tree exposure, creating a pathway for the juice to run through.
2. Next, place a container or a keg at the end of the bamboo stick in such a way that the juice runs into it. You can leave the container on the spot for a few hours or minutes in other to tap enough juice. Once the desired quantity of palm wine has been collected, use a cheesecloth to strain the wine then bottle as desired.
3. Serve.

KAI KAI
(Distilled Palm Wine)

Distilled from palm wine. Can be used to relieve sore throat.

Ingredients

1. Tapped palm wine

Instructions

1. Tapping the palm wine: when on the tree, use a sharp knife to cut out some of the palm tree leaves in other to expose the tissue then cut 10-12 cm deep into the tree. Place a hollow bamboo stick at the point of tree exposure, creating a pathway for the juice to run through.
2. Next, place a container or a keg at the end of the bamboo stick in such a way that the juice runs into it. You can leave the container on the spot for days so it can collect enough juice. The next step is the fermentation process. Pour the collected palm wine into a large drum, seal the drums with a thick nylon material and let it sit for about one week.
3. Thoroughly mix the fermented palm wine, stirring with a paddle until the thick and reddish-brown sludge is properly combined. Pour the palm wine into a large metal pot then cook for a few minutes until it boils and steam forms.
4. The steam is made to pass through a copper pipe built into a cooling barrel. Let the steam or vapour condense and drip into plastic containers while you discard the waste from the metal pot. Serve.

MMIRI UKWA
(Breadfruit Juice)

Anti-inflammatory and high in fibre. Able to aid weight loss.

Ingredients

1. 700g of ukwa (African breadfruit).

Instructions

1. Using a large mixing bowl, add in the ukwa and water to cover then let soak overnight. The next day, sieve out the ukwa, place in another bowl with clean water and wash properly. As you wash the ukwa, make sure to look out for stones, sand, and dirt at the bottom.
2. Place a pressure pot over medium heat, add in the ukwa and cover with water. Cook for about 1 hour 20 minutes until it becomes soft/tender to the touch. Once cooked, strain the liquid into serving cups. Enjoy.

ZOBO DRINK
(Hibiscus Drink)

Though not a traditional Igbo drink, but popular due to its health benefits. Known to aid weight loss, lower blood pressure and maintains healthy eye sight.

Ingredients

1. 1 cup of zobo leave (hibiscus or sorrel leaves).
2. 1 whole and sliced pineapple.
3. 1 sliced orange.
4. 2 minced ginger.
5. 4 cloves.
6. 1/4 cup of sugar or its substitute.

Instructions

1. Pour water into a cooking pot over medium heat, add in the zobo leaves alongside the grated ginger, cloves, orange, and pineapple then let boil for about 30 minutes. Once cooked, take the cooking pot out of the heat, add in the sugar or sweetener of choice then stir properly to combine.
2. Let the zobo drink cool for a few minutes then sieve using a fine mesh. Pour the zobo into a jar and chill in the fridge for a few minutes, serve.

NUTRITIONAL CONTENTS:
100g serving: calories 37, carbohydrates: 7.41g, protein: 0.43g, fat: 0.65g, fiber: 0.3

www.ingramcontent.com/pod-product-compliance
Lightning Source LLC
Chambersburg PA
CBHW051247110526
44588CB00025B/2903